I KNOW MY RIGHTS

GEORGIA

By

David W. Jackson, MSW

I Know My Rights, Georgia

ISBN: 978-1-7351867-1-9

Credits
Editorial: Carla DuPont
Cover Design: Garrett Myers
Interior Design: Carla DuPont

DEDICATION

This book is dedicated to my wife, Rhonda. Thank you for being the one to encourage me constantly and tell me that I am great. Thank you for being the one who planted the seed to write this book and constantly pushed me to get it done. You have been with me through this process and continuously encouraged me to keep going. Without your support, this would have never become a reality. Thank you and I Love You!

ACKNOWLEDGMENTS

To the South DeKalb and City of Morrow citizens, this book was written based on my experiences and interactions with you all. I hope this can be a guide in helping you all, as well as all of the great citizens in the State of Georgia, to gain a better understanding of the law and police procedures. Hopefully this book will be a pier that helps hold up the deck on this continuing bridge being built between police and citizens.

I would like to thank the late Lamont Major. Without him, I would have never become a police officer. I was working security at Northlake Mall and Lamont worked at a cellphone kiosk. He approached me one day at work and asked if I'd ever thought about being a police officer. I looked at him like he was crazy. He consistently asked me for about a week and I finally went with him to the DeKalb County Police Headquarters where we both applied. I made it in and Lamont unfortunately didn't. That was in 2011. We kept in contact up until his untimely death in 2015. I just want to say thank you to Lamont for approaching me and staying persistent. You are the reason I am still policing today. Rest well my friend.

I would like to thank all of the officers in the Warrants and Permits Office for my experience under your tutelage while I was a cadet. You all gave me some insight into what to be prepared for once the academy began. I would like to thank my classmates in DeKalb County's 94th Police Academy and Instructors Turman, Schreiner, and Rucker. You will forever be my brothers and sisters. We went through 6 months of… stuff, in order for me to be where I am today.

A special shout out to Officer J. Houston (#3128), Officer T. Johnson (#3130), Officer B. Holloman (#3127), and Officer B. Collins (#3121) for being there over the years as a solid support system whenever I needed you after graduation. I want to thank DeKalb County's South Precinct family, especially South Morning Watch and all of my primary Field Training Officers, (G. Barber, V. Daniel, and A. Green). You all helped me learn how to operate as an officer in a very high stress environment, how to be a team member, and helped to shape the premise of this book based on our numerous conversations and encounters. To Sergeant J. Bonds, Sergeant Ramey, Sergeant A. James, and Sergeant N. Hines, you are the examples I used to model myself after on how to be an effective sergeant once I got promoted. Thank you for your leadership.

I would like to thank my City of Morrow Police Department Family. Thank you to the City Manager, Sylvia Redic and Chief James Callaway for giving me the opportunity to serve the great City of Morrow. Thank you Chief, for allowing me to take the necessary measures in order to advance my policing career. Thank you to Lieutenant R. Beard. From day one you showed me that I was a valued team member. You taught me how to be a sergeant through the good and rough times we had with the team. I went from being your team member to your second-in-command. I appreciate the time you took to show me how to go to the next level.

I would like to thank the Georgia State University Class of 2017 Part-time Masters of Social Work cohort. The lessons I learned during my time in school broadened my mindset and helped me to understand where there is a need in the communities that we serve. Thank you to Cindy Stroud, MSW; Olivia Mason, MSW; Sabrina Brown, LMSW; Jewel Wakefield, MSW, LMSW; and Valerie Dunham, LMSW, LCSW-A. I would not have made it through school without you all.

I would like to thank Danielle Whylly, PhD, and the Northern District of Georgia U.S. Attorney's Office. The Real Talk About the Law program was another catalyst that pushed me to write this book. Being able to interact with at-risk youth and with current and former incarcerated individuals let me know that some of their situations could have been avoided if they had the proper information. Dr. Whylly, thank you for our many conversations on communities that need to be informed and educated on the law in order to gain a better understanding of their own actions and the actions of police. Being my mentor as a Community Outreach Specialist showed me the broader perspective of how to address issues on a larger scale and that every little bit done does matter. Thank you.

TABLE OF CONTENTS

PREFACE

This book was written to help educate all citizens in the State of Georgia. It was written to inform people of their rights and help with understanding some police procedures during interactions. The purpose is to give insight from the first hand perspective of myself, as a police officer. It outlines some of the most common citizen/police encounters that occur on a daily basis and is also based on the laws, and my interpretation of those laws, as an officer.

In my experience as a police officer, I have engaged a number of citizens in many different situations. I have found that a lot of people are very misguided and misinformed. It is also my belief that people react based on what they know or have been told. This is what has led many people to say, "I know my rights," when engaged with an officer. Some do know their rights, but most of the citizens I have encountered were either misinformed and/or not knowledgeable about the law and police procedures.

All of the information in this book is public knowledge and can be found on the various websites in the reference section. There are also apps with Georgia Law on them: Georgia Codem GA Laws, Police Guide, and US Laws. These apps allow you to have instant access to the law in the palm of your hand. Doing a Google search starting with OCGA (Official Code of Georgia Annotate), then putting in which law you want to research will lead you to many sites. The site I have used that has not failed me is the Law Justia website. For example, go to a Google search bar and type: OCGA red-light violation. This website coupled with the actual law handbook is what I used to find most of the information in all of the chapters.

I have consolidated this book into 7 chapters of the most common cases and situations that I have had to handle during my time as a police officer. I hope this book is informative and helps many of you when it comes to knowing your rights and understanding why police officers do what they do.

Thank You

So misunderstood, but yet so needed,
Feelings of joy, distress, and sometimes defeated
Knowing how we are viewed but show up to work every day,
Helping those who despise us and those who honor us in the same way,
Being judged by the few wrong because of the uniform we wear,
Knowing the public outlook on all of us is often not fair,
We know the ones who are wrong, are among the few,
But we still have to show up to do what we do,
So, from one officer to another, a sincere thank you,
Thank you: For when you have to be a fireman and put out a small flame,
Thank you: For finding that runaway and taking him or her back from where they came,
Thank you: For running to the danger when others run away,
Thank you: For not ending some roll calls until you all have prayed,
Thank you: For playing public works removing objects that are blocking the road,
Thank you: For playing code enforcement enforcing city or county codes,
Thank you: For showing compassion when you have to deliver a death notice,
Thank you: For when you are tired and fatigued and not losing focus,
Thank you: For being on call and always alert

Thank you: For pushing through the physical,
emotional, and mental pain and hurt,
Thank you: For when you have to play EMT and
render first aid,
Thank you: For being overworked and under paid,
As a fellow officer, I appreciate you all and it will take
some time,
For us to work through all of the turmoil and still have
to fight crime,
Those of us who can, let's do what we can, to try
and fix,
The way we are viewed in the public eye, and watch
your six.

I KNOW MY RIGHTS

GEORGIA

1 ASSAULT & BATTERY

There are multiple types of assaults in the Georgia Law Enforcement Handbook. One of the misconceptions is that an assault consists of physical contact between parties. This is partially true; however, this is not always the case. Here are the legal definitions of the most common types of assaults I have encountered as an officer:

O.C.G.A. 16-5-20 - Simple Assault: (a) A person commits the offense of simple assault when he or she either:(1) Attempts to commit a violent injury to the person of another; or (2) Commits an act which places another in reasonable apprehension of immediately receiving a violent injury.

O.C.G.A. 16-5-23 - Simple Battery: (a) A person commits the offense of simple battery when he or she either: (1) Intentionally makes physical contact of an insulting or provoking nature with the person of another; or (2) Intentionally causes physical harm to another.

O.C.G.A. 16-5-23.1 - Battery: (a) A person commits the offense of battery when he or she intentionally causes substantial physical harm or visible bodily harm to another. (b) As used in this Code section, the term "visible bodily harm" means bodily harm capable of being perceived by a person other than the victim and may include, but is not limited to, substantially blackened eyes, substantially swollen lips or other facial or body parts, or substantial bruises to body parts.

O.C.G.A. 16-5-21. - Aggravated Assault: (a) A person commits the offense of aggravated assault when he or she assaults: (1) With intent to murder, to rape, or to rob; (2) With a deadly weapon or with any object, device, or instrument which, when used offensively against a person, is likely to or actually does result in serious bodily injury; or (3) A person or persons without legal justification by discharging a firearm from within a motor vehicle toward a person or persons.

O.C.G.A. 16-5-24 - Aggravated Battery: (a) A person commits the offense of aggravated battery when he or she maliciously causes bodily harm to another by depriving him or her of a member of his or her body, by rendering a member of his or her body useless, or by seriously disfiguring his or her body or a member thereof.

O.C.G.A. 16-11-37 - Terroristic Threats: (a) A person commits the offense of a terroristic threat when he or she threatens to commit any crime of violence, to release any hazardous substance, as such term is defined in Code Section 12-8-92, or to burn or damage property with the purpose of terrorizing another or of causing the evacuation of a building, place of assembly, or facility of public transportation or otherwise causing serious public inconvenience or in reckless disregard of the risk of causing such terror or inconvenience. No person shall be convicted under this subsection on the uncorroborated testimony of the party to whom the threat is communicated.

O.C.G.A. 16-11-32 - Affray: (a) An affray is the fighting by two or more persons in some public place to the disturbance of the public tranquility.

SEXUAL OFFENSES

O.C.G.A. 16-6-22.1 - Sexual Battery: (a) For the purposes of this Code section, the term "intimate parts" means the primary genital area, anus, groin, inner thighs, or buttocks of a male or female and the breasts of a female. (b) A person commits the offense of sexual battery when he or she intentionally makes physical contact with the intimate parts of the body of another person without the consent of that person. (c) Except as otherwise provided in this Code section, a person convicted of the offense of sexual battery shall be punished as for a misdemeanor of a high and aggravated nature.

O.C.G.A. 16-6-22.2 - Aggravated Sexual Battery: (a) For the purposes of this Code section, the term "foreign object" means any article or instrument other than the sexual organ of a person. (b) A person commits the offense of aggravated sexual battery when he or she intentionally penetrates with a foreign object the sexual organ or anus of another person without the consent of that person.

O.C.G.A. 16-6-1 - Rape: (a) A person commits the offense of rape when he has carnal knowledge of: (1) A female forcibly and against her will; or (2) A female who is less than ten years of age.

Carnal knowledge in rape occurs when there is any penetration of the female sex organ by the male sex organ. The fact that the person allegedly raped is the wife of the defendant shall not be a defense to a charge of rape.

O.C.G.A. 16-6-2 - Sodomy and Aggravated Sodomy: (a) (1) A person commits the offense of sodomy when he or she performs or submits to any sexual act involving the sex organs of one person and the mouth or anus of another. (2) A person commits the offense of aggravated sodomy when he or she commits sodomy with force and against the will of the other person or when he or she commits sodomy with a person who is less than ten years of age. The fact that the person allegedly sodomized is the spouse of a defendant shall not be a defense to a charge of aggravated sodomy.

EXPLANATIONS

I am going to break down each of these offenses in a basic manner based on my understanding of each of the charges.

Simple Assault - **contains no physical contact**. It is verbally speaking to someone and/or making a threatening motion towards someone in a manner in which he or she perceives that his or her immediate safety is in danger.

Simple Battery - making physical contact with someone, without leaving any visible marks or injuries.

Battery - making physical contact with someone, resulting in visible bruising or injuries (Examples: scratches, lacerations, bleeding, swelling, etc.)

Aggravated Assault - Using a weapon or object in a manner that causes someone to fear for their safety or using it in a manner that a person commits the offense of battery with the weapon or object. **Does not necessarily need physical contact for this offense.** (Examples: pointing a gun at someone, shooting at someone, throwing a chair at someone, hitting someone with a bat, cutting a person with a sharp object leaving a visible superficial cut or wound)

Aggravated Battery - Causing harm to a person in a matter in which the person sustains some type of disfiguration or dismemberment. (Examples: broken arm in an attack, punching someone in the face and knocking a tooth out, breaking someone's finger)

Terroristic Threats – The most common example I see of this is when someone is in a crowd of people or in the presence of police and says to another person, "I'm gonna f..king kill you!" I have also seen an example where a married couple got into a dispute. The wife was not home and the husband sent her a text saying, "I got something for you when you get home!" and texted her a picture of the gun kept at their residence.

Affray - Two or more people in a fight in public that causes a civil disturbance. Police usually cannot definitively decide how the fight started due to a lack of neutral evidence, so both parties are charged with the crime that usually happens in the presence of the officers.

Sexual Battery - When a person touches or gropes someone's private areas *on purpose* without the other person's consent: breasts of female, inner thighs of male and female, groin of male and female (including penis on male and vagina on female), buttocks of male and female, and anus of male and female. Touching is not limited to the hands. In the code section it states "makes physical contact".

Aggravated Sexual Battery - When a person uses an object that is not a sexual organ to penetrate the vagina of a female, urethra of a male, or anus of a male or female without the consent of the battered party.

Rape - First let's define Carnal Knowledge. Carnal Knowledge is simply sexual intercourse where a male penis penetrates a female vagina. Rape is when carnal knowledge occurs without the consent of the female or the female is under ten years of age.

Sodomy - The act of sodomy is when a person performs a sexual act or allows another person to perform that act on him or her involving the mouth contacting the sexual organs of another individual or the anus of that person consensually [when the act is agreed upon between the two parties]. For example, felatio (a man having oral sex performed on him), cunnilingus (a woman having oral sex performed on her), and anal sex both male and female.

Aggravated Sodomy - When the act of sodomy is performed against the will of another person or the other person is under ten years of age.

I hope this outline helps with understanding the difference between assault and battery charges; they all do not have to involve physical contact. As for the type of charge associated with the crimes, Terroristic Threats, Aggravated Assault, Aggravated Battery, Rape, and Aggravated Sodomy are all felonies.

PROSECUTION OF ASSAULTS

When it comes to pressing charges on someone, the process is not as simple as people think. If an officer makes a lawful arrest based on an incident he did not witness, the officer is responsible for that arrest.

In assault cases and domestic situations, the officer has to determine if the evidence, testimonies, and witness accounts of the incident are valid and can help the officer determine who the primary aggressor is in the situation.

For example, in the instance of Simple Battery in a domestic situation, where either party admits that they physically assaulted the other party although there is no physical evidence, the officer can make an arrest based on that confession. If the stories are conflicting and there is no physical evidence, in my experience, the officer would give each party the case number, document the testimonies and any evidence observed. This would be followed by a report on the situation, as well as advising the individuals what actions need to be taken if either wants to pursue charges on the other. If the officer feels there is enough evidence to effect an arrest, he or she can make the arrest.

If there is a Battery case, unless witnessed in the officer's presence, the officer has to make a determination based on the evidence at the scene, witness accounts, and testimonies of all parties involved. The determination can also be made based on the extent of the injury incurred by one of the parties.

Note: Determining a primary aggressor in some situations is one of the most difficult tasks an officer has to do.

For example, in my experience, if a male and female get into a verbal altercation and the female slaps the male and scratches him leaving a visible injury, the female would be considered the primary aggressor. If the male pushes the female to get her off of him, the female would *still* be considered the primary aggressor. If the male, with a closed fist, punches the female and breaks her nose, the male would be considered the primary aggressor due to the severity of the injury he caused to the female.

Let's flip it. If the male and female get into a verbal altercation and the male pushes the female leaving no injury, the male would be the primary aggressor based on the testimonies. Unless he confesses to pushing her, it's probable no arrest would be made, but the incident should be documented. If the male pushes the female, then the female jumps on him and starts scratching his face, she now becomes the primary aggressor based on the severity of the injury she has caused.

Note: Ladies, the "he does not have the right to put his hands on a female" plea is not a law. It also is not an excuse for any of you to physically attack a male and expect him not to defend himself. If a person gets a male or female to a point where he or she feels the need to physically assault the other, the parties need to separate whether temporarily or permanently.

"BECAUSE YOU ARE A FEMALE DOES NOT AUTOMATICALLY MAKE YOU RIGHT!"

Myth Buster

I hear a lot of men say, "You are going to automatically take her side because she is a female." This is not true. The case should be judged on the totality of the circumstances, evidence, and testimonies, not on the gender of the parties. Also, **it does not matter who calls the police.** The officers will make their determination based on the evidence at the scene, testimonies, and accounts of the incident by any witnesses involved.

ONCE AGAIN, IF YOU ARE WITH SOMEONE WHO YOU HAVE TO CALL THE POLICE ON, OR GETS YOU SO UPSET THAT IT RESORTS TO VIOLENCE, THEN YOU SHOULD REALLY EVALUATE YOUR

SITUATION AND THINK ABOUT WHO YOU ARE WITH!

This section and the Domestic Violence section usually go hand-in-hand. It is very important to understand that in the State of Georgia, if there is a physical altercation and one person gets arrested on a domestic violence charge, *the other party cannot drop the charges*. The State of Georgia prosecutes domestic violence charges (See the Domestic Violence Section).

In cases where the parties do not fit the domestic statute, the victim can choose whether or not he or she wants to press charges against the violator.

If at all possible, try to record the incident, conversations, or messages to strengthen the case. It has to be understood, that unless the officers witness the actual incident, which is very rare, the officers can only make determinations and arrests based on the evidence that they are given. In this age of "no snitching", people get upset because the officers don't do what they **believe** the officers should, but at the same time will not give officers the information needed to make the proper conclusion.

Officers are responsible for every arrest they make. They have to make sure that there is probable cause and sufficient evidence to substantiate the charges for the person who is arrested. If the officer does not have sufficient probable cause for the arrest, then the arrest should not be made. Officers do not make arrests just because someone wants them to. This is not television and officers are held accountable for the reasoning behind every arrest, just like the guilty party is held accountable for the offense committed.

Do not always look to the police to solve your personal problems and do not try to use police to get pay back or scare someone. The matter will be thoroughly investigated and the proper conclusion, based on what is discovered, will be made. That conclusion may not be popular. Understand that the officer doing the investigation knows his or her name is on the line and he or she is responsible. Trying to use police to settle a personal score can get the instigator in trouble and charges can be made against him or her. One charge that could be made is Unlawful conduct during 9-1-1 call, or as known by the general public as, "abuse of 9-1-1 call."

O.C.G.A. 16-11-39.2 - Unlawful conduct during 9-1-1 call: (a) As used in this Code section, the term: (1) "Call" shall have the same meaning as set forth in paragraph (2.1) of Code Section 46-5-122. (2) ***"False report"*** *means the fabrication of an incident or crime or of material information relating to an incident or crime which the person making the report knows to be false at the time of making the report.(3)* ***"Harass"*** *means to knowingly and willingly engage in any conduct directed toward a communications officer that is likely to impede or interfere with such communications officer's duties, that threatens such communication officer or any member of his or her family, or that places any member of the public served or to be served by 9-1-1 service in danger of injury or delayed assistance.(4)* ***"Harassing"*** *means the willful use of opprobrious and abusive language which has no legitimate* *purpose in relation to imparting information relevant to an emergency call.(5)* ***"9-1-1"*** *means a public safety answering point as defined in paragraph (15) of Code Section 46-5-122. The term "9-1-1" also means the digits, address, Internet Protocol address, or other information used to access or initiate a call to a public safety answering point.*

(b) A person commits the offense of unlawful conduct during a 9-1-1 telephone call if he or she: (1) Without provocation, uses obscene, vulgar, or profane language with the intent to intimidate or harass a 9-1-1 communications officer; (2) Calls or otherwise contacts 9-1-1, whether or not conversation ensues, for the purpose of annoying, harassing, or molesting a 9-1-1 communications officer or for the purpose of interfering with or disrupting emergency telephone service; (3) Calls or otherwise contacts 9-1-1 and fails to hang up or disengage the connection for the intended purpose of interfering with or disrupting emergency service; (4) Calls or otherwise contacts 9-1-1 with the intention to harass a communications officer; or (5) Calls or otherwise contacts 9-1-1 and makes a false report.

(c) Any person who violates subsection (b) of this Code section shall be guilty of a misdemeanor and, upon conviction thereof, shall be punished by a fine of not more than $500.00 or 12 months in jail, or both.

(d) Any violation of subsection (b) of this Code section shall be considered to have been committed in any county where such call to or contact with 9-1-1 originated or in

any county where the call to or contact with 9-1-1 was received.

2 CHAPTER FOR TEENS

Although the title of this chapter specifies teens, some of the laws in this chapter apply to everyone. This chapter is to highlight different pitfalls and offenses that, in my experience, are usually committed by juvenile offenders. This section is to educate everyone on ways to help make juveniles aware of the laws concerning them and help them understand laws that they may or may not know are being broken. This chapter also informs teens and parents of the severity of punishments associated with committing crimes.

WHO IS CONSIDERED A JUVENILE?

O.C.G.A 15-11-28. Jurisdiction of juvenile court - (a) Exclusive original jurisdiction. Except as provided in subsection (b) of this Code section, the court shall have exclusive original jurisdiction over juvenile matters and shall be the sole court for initiating action: (1) Concerning any child: (A) Who is alleged to be delinquent; (B) Who is alleged to be unruly; (C) Who is alleged to be deprived; (D) Who is alleged to be in need of treatment or commitment as a mentally ill or mentally retarded child; (E) Who is alleged to have committed a juvenile traffic offense as defined in Code Section 15-11-73; or (F) Who has been placed under the supervision of the court or on probation to the court; provided, however, that such jurisdiction shall be for the sole purpose of completing, effectuating, and enforcing such supervision or a probation begun ***prior to the child's seventeenth birthday.***

It also states in this code section, that if a child between the ages of 13-17 commits a forcible felony, he or she can be charged as an adult through superior court:

O.C.G.A 15-11-28: (1) Except as provided in paragraph (2) of this subsection, the court shall have concurrent jurisdiction with the superior court over a child who is alleged to have committed a delinquent act which would be considered a crime if tried in a superior court and for which the child may be punished by loss of life, imprisonment for life without possibility of parole, or confinement for life in a penal institution.(2)(A) The superior court shall have exclusive jurisdiction over the trial of any child 13 to 17 years of age who is alleged to have committed any of the following offenses: (i) Murder; (ii) Voluntary manslaughter; (iii) Rape; (iv) Aggravated sodomy; (v) Aggravated child molestation; (vi) Aggravated sexual battery; or (vii) Armed robbery if committed with a firearm.

So according to this section of the Georgia Law Book, any child who commits an offense between the ages of 13-16 years 364 days old (or 365 depending on leap years), will be subjected to the juvenile court's jurisdiction over his or her case, unless the case is bound over or transferred to superior court. If an offense is committed the day a juvenile turns 17-years-old or after, he or she is no longer considered a juvenile and will be charged as an adult for the crime committed.

O.C.G.A 16-11-131 - Forcible Felony: (e) As used in this Code section, the term 'forcible felony' means any felony which involves the use or threat of physical force or violence against any person and further includes, without limitation, murder; felony murder; burglary; robbery; armed robbery; kidnapping; hijacking of an aircraft or motor vehicle; aggravated stalking; rape; aggravated child molestation; aggravated sexual battery; arson in the first degree; the manufacturing, transporting, distribution, or possession of explosives with intent to kill, injure, or intimidate individuals or destroy a public building; terroristic threats; or acts of treason or insurrection.

In my experience, the most common forcible felonies I have witnessed committed by juveniles, based on this definition are murder, burglary, robbery, armed robbery, hijacking of a motor vehicle (carjacking), and terroristic threats. Many of these crimes I have had dealings with involving juveniles are gang related. Many juveniles are not aware that they can be charged as adults, but as stated earlier in this section, depending on the crime, the juvenile can be charged at the age of 13.

GANG STATUTE

According to the State of Georgia, what is a gang and what is gang activity?

O.C.G.A 16-15-3 (2) "Criminal street gang": means any organization, association, or group of three or more persons associated in fact, whether formal or informal, which engages in criminal gang activity as defined in paragraph (1) of this Code section. The existence of such organization, association, or group of individuals associated in fact may be established by evidence of a common name or common identifying signs, symbols, tattoos, graffiti, or attire or other distinguishing characteristics, including, but not limited to, common activities, customs, or behaviors. Such term shall not include three or more persons, associated in fact, whether formal or informal, who are not engaged in criminal gang activity.

My understanding is that a criminal street gang is three or more people who commit a crime together and there is something between the three or more of them that shows affiliation with each other. This is not limited to known organizations. For example, three or more members of a family are at a family reunion. They go to the store and get into a dispute with employees at the store. They decide to knock over the stand with snacks on it and throw a brick through the window out of anger. They are arrested and charged with simple assault and criminal trespass. All of them are wearing family reunion t-shirts. Those shirts show affiliation with each other. Technically by law, based on the crime of simple assault and criminal trespass, these individuals can be charged as a gang according to the statute. So, what is gang activity?

O.C.G.A 16-15-3 (1) "Criminal gang activity": means the commission, attempted commission, conspiracy to commit, or solicitation, coercion, or intimidation of another person to commit any of the following offenses on or after July 1, 2006: (A) Any offense defined as racketeering activity by Code Section 16-14-3; (B) Any offense defined in Article 7 of Chapter 5 of this title, relating to stalking; (C) Any offense defined in Code Section 16-6-1 as rape, 16-6-2 as aggravated sodomy, 16-6-3 as statutory rape, or 16-6-22.2 as aggravated sexual battery; (D) Any offense defined in Article 3 of Chapter 10 of this title, relating to escape and other offenses related to confinement; (E) Any offense defined in Article 4 of Chapter 11 of this title, relating to dangerous instrumentalities and practices; (F) Any offense defined in Code Section 42-5-15, 42-5-16, 42-5-17, 42-5-18, or 42-5-19, relating to the security of state or county correctional facilities; (G) Any offense defined in Code Section 49-4A-11, relating to aiding or encouraging a child to escape from custody; (H) Any offense of criminal trespass or criminal damage to property resulting from any act of gang related painting on, tagging, marking on, writing on, or creating any form of graffiti on the property of another; (I) Any criminal offense committed in violation of the laws of the United States or its territories, dominions, or possessions, any of the several states, or any foreign nation which, if committed in this state, would be considered criminal gang activity under this Code section; and (J) Any criminal offense in the State of Georgia, any other state, or the United States that involves violence, possession of a weapon, or use of a weapon, whether designated as a felony or not, and regardless of the maximum sentence that could be imposed or actually was imposed.

<u>*O.C.G.A 16-15-4. Participation in criminal gang activity prohibited:*</u> *(a) It shall be unlawful for any person employed by or associated with a criminal street gang to conduct or participate in criminal gang activity through the commission of any offense enumerated in paragraph (1) of Code Section 16-15-3. (b) It shall be unlawful for any person to commit any offense enumerated in paragraph (1) of Code Section 16-15-3 with the intent to obtain or earn membership or maintain or increase his or her status or position in a criminal street gang. (c) It shall be unlawful for any person to acquire or maintain, directly or indirectly, through criminal gang activity or proceeds derived therefrom any interest in or control of any real or personal property of any nature, including money.*

<u>*(k) (1) Any person who violates subsection (a), (b), or (c) of this Code section shall, in addition to any other penalty imposed by law, be punished by imprisonment for not less than five nor more than 15 years or by a fine of not less than $10,000.00 nor more than $15,000.00, or both.*</u>

LET'S DO SOME MATH!

These calculations are strictly according to what the law book dictates. Judges have the authority to choose punishment as they see fit according to the law. Charges can be reduced or dropped during the court process. These numbers are estimated based on whether or not the accused party is convicted.

Let's take a common offense committed by juveniles, burglary; in this example it will be the first offense. In committing a burglary, one would likely force entry into a location and use some type of tools to do so. When the alarm is set off, the police are alerted. The police arrive, the suspects get in a car and flee from the scene. During the chase the suspects are driving 60 mph down a residential street marked at 35 mph. After the chase, the three suspects are caught. They are in possession of a backpack with stolen goods and in the backpack is a small pry bar, large screw drivers, and gloves. One suspect is 17, one is 15, and, one is 14-years-old. They are wearing red bandanas and have admitted to being a part of the Bloods street gang.

The offenses in a case like this would be as follows: Burglary, Criminal Damage to Property, Possession of tools of the crime, and Fleeing and Eluding.

Crime	Min Sentence	Max Sentence
Burglary 1st degree	1 year	20 years
Criminal Damage 2nd degree	1 year	5 years
Possession of Tools	1 year	5 years
Fleeing and Eluding	1 year	5 years
Total	**4 years**	**35 years**

Without the gang statute the suspects are looking at 4-35 years for the burglary. Adding the gang statute according to 16-15-4(k):

Crime	Min Sentence	Max Sentence
Burglary 1st degree	6 years	35 years
Criminal Damage 2nd degree	6 years	20 years
Possession of Tools	6 years	20 years
Fleeing and Eluding	6 years	20 years
Total	**24 years**	**95 years**

The 14-year-old is facing a sentence that could have him incarcerated until he is 38 -109 years old. The 15-year-old is facing a sentence that could have him incarcerated until he is 39-110 years old. The 17-year-old is facing a sentence that could have him incarcerated until he is 41-112 years old.

I am not stating that this is the amount of time that these individuals will be incarcerated. What I am stating is that based on the crimes committed, this is the punishment they are subjecting themselves to according to the law. There may be programs in place for the 14 and 15-year-old, but the 17-year old is considered an adult and not subject to the juvenile court system proceedings.

SEXTING

What is sexting? Sexting is the sending, receiving, or forwarding of sexually explicit materials of oneself or others by using digital media including cellphones, computers, and other digital devices. Sending someone naked pictures or videos mainly of the sender. This can be with or without consent. The reason I am putting sexting in this chapter is because there are different consequences for juveniles sending and receiving nude media to each other.

My understanding of these laws is as follows:

Any child under the age of 18 is considered a juvenile under these laws. If said juvenile takes a picture/video of his or herself in his or her phone while under the age of 18, they are now in possession of child pornography. If said juvenile sends a picture/video to his or her girlfriend or boyfriend, said juvenile has now distributed child pornography. Because cell towers cross state lines, these charges are no longer state jurisdictional but federal.

"In the case, Jane Doe used the phone-based application Snapchat to send a revealing selfie to a boy at her school in Southern Minnesota. He went on to make a copy and distribute it to other students without Jane's permission. Even though Jane didn't victimize anybody, Rice County's prosecutor charged her with felony distribution of child pornography. A conviction, or even a guilty plea to a lesser charge, would require Jane to spend 10 years on the sex offender registry." (Nelson, 2018)

In my experience, most of these cases, dealing with teenagers originate from teens breaking up with each other and one trying to get back at another, teens wanting to brag to their friends about who they are having sex with, or parents who do not want their child dating an individual and find pictures in said child's phone and want to press charges. There are other ways these cases develop; here are some common ones.

The federal statutes that govern these charges are as follows:

18 U.S.C. § 2251 - Sexual Exploitation of Children-(Production of child pornography)

18 U.S.C. § 2251A - Selling and Buying of Children
18 U.S.C. § 2252- Certain activities relating to material involving the sexual exploitation of minors-(Possession, distribution and receipt of child pornography)
18 U.S.C. § 2252A - certain activities relating to material constituting or containing child pornography

18 U.S.C. § 2256 - Definitions

18 U.S.C. § 2260 - Production of sexually explicit depictions of a minor for importation into the United States

Images of child pornography are not protected under First Amendment rights and are illegal contraband under federal law. Section 2256 of Title 18, United States Code, defines child pornography as any visual depiction of sexually explicit conduct involving a minor (someone under 18 years of age). Visual depictions include photographs, videos, digital or computer generated images indistinguish-able from an actual minor, and images created, adapted, or modified, but appear to depict an identifiable, actual minor. Undeveloped film, undeveloped videotape, and electronically stored data that can be converted into a visual image of child pornography are also deemed illegal visual depictions under federal law.

Notably, the legal definition of sexually explicit conduct does not require that an image depict a child engaging in sexual activity. A picture of a naked child may constitute illegal child pornography if it is sufficiently sexually suggestive. Additionally, the age of consent for sexual activity in a given state is irrelevant; any depiction of a minor under 18 years of age engaging in sexually explicit conduct is illegal.

Federal law prohibits the production, distribution, reception, and possession of an image of child pornography using or affecting any means or facility of interstate or foreign commerce (See 18 U.S.C. § 2251; 18 U.S.C. § 2252; 18 U.S.C. § 2252A). Specifically, Section 2251 makes it illegal to persuade, induce, entice, or coerce a minor to engage in sexually explicit conduct for purposes of producing visual depictions of that conduct. Any individual who attempts or conspires to commit a child pornography offense is also subject to prosecution under federal law.

Federal jurisdiction is implicated if the child pornography offense occurred in interstate or foreign commerce. This includes, for example, using the U.S. Mail or common carriers to transport child pornography across state or international borders. Additionally, federal jurisdiction almost always applies when the internet is used to commit a child pornography violation. Even if the child pornography image itself did not travel across state or international borders, federal law may be implicated if the materials, such as the computer used to download the image or the CD-ROM used to store the image originated or previously traveled in interstate or foreign commerce.

In addition, Section 2251A of Title 18, United States Code, specifically prohibits any parent, legal guardian or other person in custody or control of a minor under the age of 18, to buy, sell, or transfer custody of that minor for purposes of producing child pornography.

Lastly, Section 2260 of Title 18, United States Code, prohibits any persons outside of the United States to knowingly produce, receive, transport, ship, or distribute child pornography with intent to import or transmit the visual depiction into the United States.

Any violation of federal child pornography law is a serious crime, and convicted offenders face severe statutory penalties. For example, a first time offender convicted of producing child pornography under 18 U.S.C. § 2251, faces fines and a statutory minimum of 15-to-30 years maximum in prison. A first time offender convicted of transporting child pornography in interstate or foreign commerce under 18 U.S.C. § 2252, faces fines and a statutory minimum of 5 years to 20 years maximum in prison. Convicted offenders may face harsher penalties if the offender has prior convictions or if the child pornography offense occurred in aggravated situations defined as (i) the images are violent, sadistic, or masochistic in nature, (ii) the minor was sexually abused, or (iii) the offender has prior convictions for child sexual exploitation. In these circumstances, a convicted offender may face up to life imprisonment.

It is important to note that an offender can be prosecuted under state child pornography laws in addition to, or instead of, federal law. (United States Department of Justice)

The State of Georgia laws governing this statute are as follows:

O.C.G.A. 16-12-100.2. Computer or electronic pornography and child exploitation prevention: (a) This Code section shall be known and may be cited as the "Computer or Electronic Pornography and Child Exploitation Prevention Act of 2007." (b) As used in this Code section, the term: (1) "Child" means any person under the age of 16 years.

(2) "Electronic device" means any device used for the purpose of communicating with a child for sexual purposes or any device used to visually depict a child engaged in sexually explicit conduct, store any image or audio of a child engaged in sexually explicit conduct, or transmit any audio or visual image of a child for sexual purposes. Such term may include, but shall not be limited to, a computer, cellular phone, thumb drive, video game system, or any other electronic device that can be used in furtherance of exploiting a child for sexual purposes; (3) "Identifiable child" means a person: (A) Who was a child at the time the visual depiction was created, adapted, or modified or whose image as a child was used in creating, adapting, or modifying the visual depiction; and (B) Who is recognizable as an actual person by the person's face, likeness, or other distinguishing characteristic, such as a unique birthmark or other recognizable feature or by electronic or scientific means as may be available. The term shall not be construed to require proof of the actual identity of the child.

(4) "Sadomasochistic abuse" has the same meaning as provided in Code Section 16-12-100.1.

(5) "Sexual conduct" has the same meaning as provided in Code Section 16-12-100.1.

(6) "Sexual excitement" has the same meaning as provided in Code Section 16-12-100.1.

(7) "Sexually explicit nudity" has the same meaning as provided in Code Section 16-12-102.

(8) "Visual depiction" means any image and includes undeveloped film and video tape and data stored on computer disk or by electronic means which is capable of conversion into a visual image or which has been created, adapted, or modified to show an identifiable child engaged in sexually explicit conduct. (c)

(1) A person commits the offense of computer or electronic pornography if such person intentionally or willfully: (A) Compiles, enters into, or transmits by computer or other electronic device; (B) Makes, prints, publishes, or reproduces by other computer or other electronic device; (C) Causes or allows to be entered into or transmitted by computer or other electronic device; or (D) Buys, sells, receives, exchanges, or disseminates any notice, statement, or advertisement, or any child's name, telephone number, place of residence, physical characteristics, or other descriptive or identifying information for the purpose of offering or soliciting sexual conduct of or with an identifiable child or the visual depiction of such conduct.

(2) Any person convicted of violating paragraph (1) of this subsection shall be punished by a fine of not more than $10,000.00 and by imprisonment for not less than one nor more than 20 years. (d) (1) It shall be unlawful for any person intentionally or willfully to utilize a computer on-line service or Internet service, including but not limited to a local bulletin board service, Internet chat room, e-mail, on-line messaging service, or other electronic device, to seduce, solicit, lure, or entice, or attempt to seduce, solicit, lure, or entice a child or another person believed by such person to be a child to commit any illegal act described in

Code Section 16-6-2, relating to the offense of sodomy or aggravated sodomy; Code Section 16-6-4, relating to the offense of child molestation or aggravated child molestation; Code Section 16-6-5, relating to the offense of enticing a child for indecent purposes; or Code Section 16-6-8, relating to the offense of public indecency or to engage in any conduct that by its nature is an unlawful sexual offense against a child.

(2) Any person who violates paragraph (1) of this subsection shall be guilty of a felony and, upon conviction thereof, shall be punished by imprisonment for not less than one nor more than 20 years and by a fine of not more than $25,000.00; provided, however, that, if at the time of the offense the victim was 14 or 15 years of age and the defendant was no more than three years older than the victim, then the defendant shall be guilty of a misdemeanor of a high and aggravated nature.

(e) (1) A person commits the offense of obscene Internet contact with a child if he or she has contact with someone he or she knows to be a child or with someone he or she believes to be a child via a computer on-line service or Internet service, including but not limited to a local bulletin board service, Internet chat room, e-mail, or on-line messaging service, and the contact involves any matter containing explicit verbal descriptions or narrative accounts of sexually explicit nudity, sexual conduct, sexual excitement, or sadomasochistic abuse that is intended to arouse or satisfy the sexual desire of either the child or the person, provided that no conviction shall be had for a

violation of this subsection on the unsupported testimony of a child.

(2) Any person who violates paragraph (1) of this subsection shall be guilty of a felony and, upon conviction thereof, shall be punished by imprisonment for not less than one nor more than ten years or by a fine of not more than $10,000.00; provided, however, that, if at the time of the offense the victim was 14 or 15 years of age and the defendant was no more than three years older than the victim, then the defendant shall be guilty of a misdemeanor of a high and aggravated nature.

(f) (1) It shall be unlawful for any owner or operator of a computer on-line service, Internet service, local bulletin board service, or other electronic device that is in the business of providing a service that may be used to sexually exploit a child to intentionally or willfully to permit a subscriber to utilize the service to commit a violation of this Code section, knowing that such person intended to utilize such service to violate this Code section. No owner or operator of a public computer on-line service, Internet service, local bulletin board service, or other electronic device that is in the business of providing a service that may be used to sexually exploit a child shall be held liable on account of any action taken in good faith in providing the aforementioned services.

(2) Any person who violates paragraph (1) of this subsection shall be guilty of a misdemeanor of a high and aggravated nature.

(g) The sole fact that an undercover operative or law enforcement officer was involved in the detection and investigation of an offense under this Code section shall not constitute a defense to prosecution under this Code section.

(h) A person is subject to prosecution in this state pursuant to Code Section 17-2-1, relating to jurisdiction over crimes and persons charged with commission of crimes generally, for any conduct made unlawful by this Code section which the person engages in while:

(1) Either within or outside of this state if, by such conduct, the person commits a violation of this Code section which involves a child who resides in this state or another person believed by such person to be a child residing in this state; or

(2) Within this state if, by such conduct, the person commits a violation of this Code section which involves a child who resides within or outside this state or another person believed by such person to be a child residing within or outside this state.

(i) Any violation of this Code section shall constitute a separate offense.

Parents please monitor your child's digital activity. Some of their actions can get them into a lot trouble that will have very costly and lifelong affects. Please review the laws above so that you and your child/children understand how costly it may be do something that may seem harmless.

TRUANCY

Truancy is the act of staying away from school without a good or valid reason. Although truancy involves the attendance of the child in school, parents can be held legally responsible and charged accordingly for the actions of their child/children.

The Georgia Department of Education states that:

As of July 1, 2004, Georgia's Compulsory School Attendance Law 20-2-690.1 became much stricter in regard to truancy. ***The new law states that more than five (5) unexcused absences constitute truancy.*** *The law also states that possible consequences for parent(s)/guardian(s) of students whose unexcused absences exceed five (5) days may be: a) At least a $25 and not more than a $100 fine, b) Up to 30 days of jail time, c) Community service, or d) Any combination of these penalties.*

Beginning the 2004-05 school year, the school will make a reasonable attempt to contact the family each day a student is absent. The school will accept excuses from parents/guardians for five (5) total days of absence each semester and will use the Georgia Board of Education Rules above to determine whether the absence is excused or unexcused. A parent can write an excuse for five (5) total days each semester, but after five (5) total days each semester, a medical excuse will be required from a doctor or other qualified medical practitioner.

At three (3) unexcused absences, the school will mail a notice to the family, requesting that a family member schedule a meeting with school staff to resolve the absence status of the student. If the student reaches five (5) unexcused absences, the family will receive a hand-delivered or certified letter with official notification that any further unexcused absences will result in charges being filed as required by state law and local protocols. The letter may be delivered as described below.

Truancy Intervention meetings will be held with parents and students when they reach the 5th unexcused absence. The meeting will be for the purpose of intervening and helping the parents find solutions to the problem of truancy in their family. The meetings will be on the first Monday of each month beginning in September and on Mondays as needed throughout the month.

Certain unexcused educational absences may be permitted without the make-up work penalty, provided arrangements are made with the local school administration prior to the absence. Family vacations are not excused absences in accordance with State of Georgia Board of Education rules. If the student accumulates three unexcused tardies to school, three unexcused check-outs, or any combination of the two, this will constitute one unexcused absence for truancy purposes only. Unexcused tardies and check-outs can be defined as convenience tardies or check-outs.

If a student wishes to obtain an employment certificate (worker's permit), the student must obtain a letter from the school principal indicating that he/she is enrolled in school full-time and has an attendance record in good standing for the academic year.

If a driver is younger than 18 years of age, a driver's permit or license can only be received if the student is enrolled in and not under suspension from school and has satisfied relevant attendance requirements for a period of one academic year prior to his/her application. If a student has more than ten school days of unexcused absences (cumulative) in any semester, the school system will submit a Certificate of Non-Compliance to the Department of Motor Vehicles (DMV) and the student's license will be revoked by the DMV.

If a student under 18 drops out of school without graduating and has remained out of school for ten consecutive days, the school system will submit a Certificate of Non-Compliance to the Department of Motor Vehicles and the student's license will be revoked by the DMV.

(Georgia Department of Education, Polk High School Handbook. 1 Jul 2004)

JUVENILE PETITION PROCESS

This section describes the process in which a petition is filed against a juvenile. A juvenile petition is equal to a warrant being taken out on an adult. This is the process as described by the State of Georgia Department of Juvenile Justice.

The criminal justice system can seem complex to those who are unfamiliar with it. To aid in your understanding, we've described here for you.

When a child under the age of 17 commits a delinquent act (a crime, if committed by an adult) or an unruly act (runaway, truancy, curfew, etc.,) a complaint is filed in the Juvenile Court. A police officer, parent, or private citizen can file a complaint, which is the equivalent of an adult arrest warrant. When the complaint is filed, a Juvenile Court intake officer decides whether or not to detain the youth based on circumstances related to the law.

If the case is a misdemeanor, or involves an unruly act, and is the child's first offense, the Court typically handles the case informally and the child is not required to appear before a judge. However, a judge has final approval of all agreements between the defense lawyer and prosecutor. There are several ways to handle a case informally:

Conferencing: All parties involved meet under the guidance of a trained, unbiased facilitator to reach an agreement satisfactory to all parties.

Informal Adjustment: A court officer gives the child certain conditions to abide by for a specific period of time and if all conditions are met, the case is withdrawn.

If the case is not handled informally, the District Attorney's Office reviews the complaint, police reports and witness statements, then files a petition. Once a petition is filed, the Court schedules an arraignment hearing where the child learns about the exact charges against him/her and what his or her constitutional rights are. The child appears before *a judge and enters a formal plea to the charges (guilty or not guilty).*

If the child denies the charge(s) at arraignment, the Court schedules an Adjudicatory hearing (the equivalent to an adult trial). Witnesses and victims are subpoenaed to appear for the adjudication. Their testimony is very important to the case because it can convey the impact of a crime on an individual or a community. Victim Assistance Advocates from the District Attorney's Office are available to support and encourage victims before and after their testimony. Juvenile Court has a separate waiting room for victims.

After all the testimony and evidence is presented, the judge either adjudicates the juvenile as a delinquent (the adult equivalent of conviction) or dismisses the petition (the adult equivalent of an acquittal).

If the child admits guilt at the arraignment or is adjudicated delinquent, then the hearing transitions into a Dispositional hearing (the adult equivalent to sentencing) and the judge pronounces the sentence and order of the Court.

Dispositions can include:

Probation with general and specific conditions:

- *Commitment to a DJJ (Department of Juvenile Justice) program or detention facility*
- *Making restitution payments to the victim*
- *Performing community service hours*
- *Paying supervision fees*

- *Suspension of driving privileges*
- *Restorative group conferencing*
- *Other outcomes deemed appropriate by the judge*

3 CHILD CUSTODY

Another hot topic when responding to domestic calls is child custody. There are many variables that come into play when addressing child custody. In my experience, there is usually a dispute when one parent violates a custody order, when parents have verbal agreements that are broken in reference to visitation, and/or one parent wants to use a child as leverage to get what he or she wants from the other parent.

In this chapter, I am going to outline what is stated by law in reference to parental and custodial issues. I am not going to breakdown the entire code section but this information and more can be found under Title 19 in the Official Code of Georgia Annotate (OCGA).

WHO HAS CUSTODY?

<u>O.C.G.A. 19-7-1. In whom parental power lies; how such power lost; recovery for homicide of child</u>: (a) Until a child reaches the age of 18 or becomes emancipated, the child shall remain under the control of his or her parents, who are entitled to the child's services and the proceeds of the child's labor. In the event that a court has awarded custody of the child to one parent, only the parent who has custody of the child is entitled to the child's services and the proceeds of the child's labor.(b) Parental power shall be lost by:(1) Voluntary contract releasing the right to a third person;(2) Consent to the adoption of the child by a third person;(3) Failure to provide necessaries for the child or abandonment of the child;(4) Consent to the child's receiving the proceeds of his own labor, which consent shall be revocable at any time;(5) Consent to the marriage of the child, who thus assumes inconsistent responsibilities; or(6) Cruel treatment of the child. (b.1) Notwithstanding subsections (a) and (b) of this Code section or any other law to the contrary, in any action involving the custody of a child between the parents or either parent and a third party limited to grandparent, great-grandparent, aunt, uncle, great aunt, great uncle, sibling, or adoptive parent, parental power may be lost by the parent, parents, or any other person if the court hearing the issue of custody, in the exercise of its sound discretion and taking into consideration all the circumstances of the case, determines that an award of custody to such third party is for the best interest of the child or children and will best promote their

welfare and happiness. There shall be a rebuttable presumption that it is in the best interest of the child or children for custody to be awarded to the parent or parents of such child or children, but this presumption may be overcome by a showing that an award of custody to such third party is in the best interest of the child or children. The sole issue for determination in any such case shall be what is in the best interest of the child or children.

To sum this section up, until a child turns 18 or is legally emancipated or there is some form of abuse or abandonment, the parent(s) have custody of the child. This section also highlights how a custodian can lose custody and who can be a third party custodian.

SIDENOTE: THE AGE OF 18, IN THIS SECTION, IS CONCERNING CUSTODY. IN THE EVENT AN INDIVIDUAL COMMITS A CRIME AT THE AGE OF 17 HE OR SHE IS CHARGED AS AN ADULT.

O.C.G.A. 19-7-2. Parents' obligations to child: It is the joint and several duty of each parent to provide for the maintenance, protection, and education of his or her child until the child reaches the age of majority, dies, marries, or becomes emancipated, whichever first occurs, except as otherwise authorized and ordered pursuant to subsection (e) of Code Section 19-6-15 and except to the extent that the duty of the parents is otherwise or further defined by court order.

I have investigated cases where a parent has tried to give their child over to police officers because he or she does not want to continue to deal with a child's disrespectful behavior. As a parent, I understand that being disrespected by your children is very frustrating, but, it is not illegal. When a child becomes disrespectful, parents will have to find other means to address the behavioral issues of the child. Unless there is a crime that has been committed by the child, an officer's involvement is very limited. Please do not call the police trying to scare the child. I have seen this tactic rendered useless and sometimes escalates the problem.

Bottom line, children are the responsibility of the parents or legal custodians. There is a process that has to be followed in order to surrender a child to the state, but it can be a lengthy process and during the process the parents/ custodians still have to deal with the child and his or her behavior. There are community resources that are available to assist with these types of situations, and parents/custodians should try to use them when and if possible.

I encourage parents/custodians who are having these issues to contact their local juvenile court system to find out the process to the start a juvenile petition on the child. Also look for local social workers, group home, and teen and adolescent treatment centers for resources.

HOW IS CUSTODY ESTABLISHED?

One of the many misconceptions about custody, especially by fathers, is the perception that because you got a female pregnant, and she has the child, you have rights to the child. Although the child may be biologically yours, unless that child is legitimized, legally, the father has no rights. The only way the father has rights is if he is married to the female when she gives birth, if he marries the female after the child is born and claims the child, has legally adopted the child, or if the father goes through the process of getting a DNA test and files the proper paperwork to prove legitimacy. The marriage right can be disproved if there is a DNA test to prove that another male is the biological father.

O.C.G.A. 19-7-20. What children are legitimate; disproving legitimacy; legitimation by marriage of parents and recognition of child: (a) All children born in wedlock or within the usual period of gestation thereafter are legitimate. (b) The legitimacy of a child born as described in subsection (a) of this Code section may be disputed. Where possibility of access exists, the strong presumption is in favor of legitimacy and the proof must be clear to establish the contrary. If pregnancy existed at the time of the marriage and a divorce is sought and obtained on that ground, the child, although born in wedlock, will not be legitimate. (c) The marriage of the mother and reputed father of a child born out of wedlock and the recognition by the father of the child as his shall render the child legitimate; in such case the child shall immediately take the surname of his father.

O.C.G.A. 19-7-25: In whom parental power over child born out of wedlock lies: ***Only the mother of a child born out of wedlock*** *is entitled to custody of the child, unless the father* *legitimates the child as provided in Code Section **19-7-21.1** or **19-7-22.** Otherwise, the mother may exercise all parental power over the child.*

O.C.G.A. 19-7-21.1: Acknowledgment of legitimation" and "legal father" defined; signing acknowledgment of legitimation; when acknowledgment not recognized; making false statement; rescinding acknowledgment: (a) As used in this Code section, the term: (1) "Acknowledgment of legitimation" means a written statement contained in a voluntary acknowledgment of paternity form indicating that a mother and father of a child born out of wedlock have freely agreed and consented that the child may be legitimated. (2) "Legal father" means a male who: (A) Has legally adopted a child; (B) Was married to the biological mother of that child at the time the child was conceived or was born, unless such paternity was disproved by a final order pursuant to Article 3 of this chapter; (C) Married the legal mother of the child after the child was born and recognized the child as his own, unless such paternity was disproved by a final order pursuant to Article 3 of this chapter; (D) Has been determined to be the father by a final paternity order pursuant to Article 3 of this chapter; (E) Has legitimated the child by a final order pursuant to Code Section 19-7-22; or (F) Has legitimated a child pursuant to this Code section and who has not surrendered or had terminated his rights to the child.

The bottom line is that when a child is born out of wedlock, the father has no rights to the child unless he, (a) marries the mother afterward and claims the child, (b) has the child legitimized, or (c) adopts the child.

After the father is legally acknowledged as having rights, both parties should get a legally binding parenting plan done. The parenting plan outlines some of the parents' involvement with a child. Subjects that can be outlined in the parenting plan vary from child care, health care, and most importantly, visitation. It can be stipulated which parent has the child on what days, hours, holidays, etc. As an officer, this is vital when we interact with couples in situations addressing child custody issues. We are law enforcement, so a legally signed document by a judge is a lawful document. Therefore, that document is the law in that case so we can enforce it. If there is no documentation presented and/or unless an officer feels as if the child may be in danger with its mother, the mother will be given possession of the child in these situations. This also applies to grandparents who may have been taking care of a child in the absence of the mother but have no paperwork to show they have custody.

Let's say officers find that a mother is unfit to care for the child. If the father has nothing to show that he is the legitimate father of the child, the child will be turned over to Child Protective Services and they can make a decision on who gets custody of the child. Police Officers are not in the position to make custody decisions without legal documentation. If an officer turns a child over to someone without the proper paperwork in place, and something happens to that child the officer will be held liable. In situations like this, the officer's priority is the safety of the child and the officer should contact the proper state officiating service that deals with custodial issues.

Parents please do not use your children as bargaining tools to manipulate the other parent. I implore all parents especially fathers, get the proper paperwork to prove custody so you have rights to your children. Fathers and mothers should make out a parenting plan and have it signed off by a judge. This way if one parent does not hold up to his or her end of the plan, he or she will be held liable by the courts. During my experience in dealing with custody issues, I have never seen verbal agreements work out according to what the parents have said between each other.

In conclusion, make the child the priority. Be man or woman enough to know your shortcomings and look out for the best interest of the child. The relationship between the parents, "should" not reflect on the safety and well-being of the child.

4 CRIMINAL PROCEDURES

In this chapter, I will outline some of the provisions behind the actions of officers as explained in Title 17 (Criminal Procedures) in the Georgia Law Enforcement Handbook and I will also share some of the factors that deal with use of force as I was trained.

COMMON QUESTIONS AND STATEMENTS

Why are police officers allowed to do what they do?

What that officer did was not necessary!

They just do what they want to do!

You can't go through my things!

Why are you searching my car?

These are some of the most common questions and statements heard throughout society today as people view police officers carrying out their duties. I have viewed countless videos of police and citizen interactions. In some of them, the police are absolutely in the wrong, according to my training and understanding of policing procedures, and many have abused their authority. In other situations, the officers operated within the scope of their given authority and the public's lack of understanding police procedures has led to a massive outcry in many communities. In some of the videos observed, I have heard citizens make statements like, "I know my rights", "I don't have to do what you say", "that's not a crime", and "you can't make me do anything." In some instances, the citizen is correct, in other instances the citizen is not correct based on criminal procedures.

JUDGMENTS AND PUNISHMENTS

Another factor that has continued to fuel the discord between civilians and police (other than the media) is the judgments and punishments, or lack thereof, handed down by judges in courts. One of the major reasons many people are upset with the legal system is the lack of what is viewed as **equal justice** and/or **equal punishments** for different people who commit the same crimes. There is a vast difference in the punishments handed down in the courts by judges for those crimes. One thing that has to be taken into account is that the same crime in different states does not automatically mean the same punishment. This book is written based on Georgia Law. Each state has laws that judges use to hand out punishments in their respective jurisdictions. As you will read further in this chapter, each judge is allowed to exercise his or her discretion when it comes to punishments based on the stipulations they are given by the law.

Police officers are most civilian's first line and only contact with a representative of the law; therefore, a lot of the backlash of what is done in courts is projected on officers. I hear a lot of people say that the law is broken. In my opinion, that is not necessarily true. The law is nothing more than a set of rules put in place to ensure there is some standard of living for everyone in this systematic society. Historically, there have been laws that were put in place to ensure a certain standard of living for many white people and reinforced a substandard of living for many blacks in this country, i.e. Jim Crow Laws. The remnant of that prejudicial system still exists in some of the governing bodies that rule over certain jurisdictions in this country, but most laws I have seen broken during my tenure as a police officer have no prejudicial connotations.

I also hear people, in the legal community, say that "Justice is Blind." I disagree with that statement. If you look at the image used to depict that quote, in my opinion, the image really says, "***Justice is Blindfolded.***" To me this means it is subjective to whoever interprets the law. When a person is blind, he or she can see no color, race, sex, gender, or nationality. Punishment for a crime would be based on the crime committed and not on who committed the crime; therefore, ensuring equal justice across the board for the same crime. However, when a person is blindfolded, the blindfold can be taken off exposing a person to his or her implicit bias and internal prejudices. This can sway his or her judgments based on whatever life experiences he or she has encountered or on how he or she feels during the time of the encounter. The biggest issue I see is not the law itself but how the person enforcing the law determines the punishment for the crime. The punishments for the written laws leave a lot of leeway for enforcing entities to decide which punishments and how punishments are handed out. For example, if a certain offense warrants a punishment of 5-10 years of confinement, how does a judge determine if a person gets the minimum or the maximum?

As stated, I believe what is flawed is the decision-making process of some of the officials who enforce the law. Police officers, sheriffs, and judges are human and have emotions, attitudes (both good and bad), implicit biases, prejudices, and personalities. Officers of the law are held to a higher standard when it comes to the enforcement of the law and how one conducts his or herself as professionals, but no one is exempt from being human. This factor is also outlined covertly in some of the laws where it asked if the officer acted in a manner in which a "reasonable" person would.

SIDENOTE

Just because citizens are not sworn law enforcement officers, does not mean they should not conduct themselves in a professional manner when encountering law enforcement **and most importantly each other.**

A person does not need to be sworn in as a law enforcement officer in order to act as if he or she has dignity, self-pride, and self-respect, for his or herself, his or her environment, and with each other. Having a high personal standard in which individuals use to govern themselves could eliminate a lot of police interaction. The law was created to govern the lawless, and does not dictate a very high standard of living. If someone has a personal standard or internal moral compass, that he or she lives by that is higher than what the law provides, he or she should have fewer interactions with law enforcement, therefore limiting encounters between themselves and law officials.

The law itself is very general and leaves room for expansion or stipulations depending on the enforcing jurisdiction. For example, the State of Georgia code for Cruelty to Animals is 16-12-4, Clayton County Ordinance for Cruelty to Animals is Sec. 14-166, and the City of Morrow Ordinance for Cruelty to Animals is Sec. 11-3-11. The city is in the county and the county is in the state. The county and city can use the state law to formulate its own ordinance under its respective jurisdiction. Each of these laws and ordinances may have a variation of the same charge but is customized for that enforcing jurisdiction.

DISCRETION

Another area, in which a lot of people are misinformed is officer discretion. Let me answer this question, what is discretion? Discretion is the freedom to decide what should be done in a particular situation. **Discretion is not a right**. It is the officer deciding how he or she chooses to enforce a particular infraction within the confines of the authority that he or she is given. Officers, lawyers, and judges use discretion to decide on an end result of a given situation.

For example, a crime like burglary constitutes a punishment of 5 years up to 20 years of confinement. The judge has the authority to choose the amount of time, within those parameters, that a person will serve in confinement. The amount of time given is at the judge's discretion based on whatever process he or she uses to hand out sufficient punishments for law breakers. Lawyers have the discretion to ask a judge to change a charge to a lesser charge or give recommendations of punishment for certain crimes.

Police also have a level of discretion when it comes to certain violations like, traffic offenses. After initiating a traffic stop for certain violations, an officer can choose to write a ticket, give a written warning, or give someone a verbal warning. In some situations, based on the offense, officers cannot exercise discretion based on the law and liability such as, driving a vehicle with no insurance (OCGA 40-6-10). An officer cannot allow a vehicle to travel on the roads in Georgia knowing that the vehicle is not insured. If the officer allows the driver to leave with the vehicle and the driver causes an accident, the officer can be held responsible for that incident. The officer can also be sued and held liable for releasing the vehicle knowing it did not have valid insurance. What an officer can do, instead of impounding the vehicle is he or she can allow the driver/owner to obtain insurance while on the traffic stop. That process can be timely and it is at the officer's discretion if he or she wants to give the driver/owner time to obtain valid insurance before releasing the driver and the vehicle. If valid insurance cannot be obtained then the vehicle will be taken to impound.

Discretionary choices can range from the type of law that is broken, based on a person's attitude and demeanor when in contact with an official, or if the violator is a repeat offender. In either instance, judges, lawyers, and law enforcement officers are acting within the parameters of their given authority. Citizens must understand that every interaction with a law enforcement authority will be different and cannot expect positive results all the time. Some officials make choices strictly based on the law while others may be more empathetic to a situation and will cut someone a break. Either way it's all done within the scope of the officiating party's authority and the law.

Now, I know some people would say that is not fair or not right, or that is too much power for a person to have over another, but the law is going to be enforced regardless. If there was no room for the officials to be lenient, then max judgments would be given out all of the time. The law gives leeway to enforcing entities, so I will reiterate again that, **discretion is the choice of the law enforcement enforcer, not a right to offenders!**

SIDENOTE: If an individual feels his or her rights were violated or the interaction was intrusive and unprofessional, I implore that person to first research the law that was broken. Read it and do a self-analysis to see if you were in the wrong based on the written law. If there is still an issue or if an individual feels he or she was treated wrongly, then follow the correct procedures to file a formal complaint with the agency the officer represents. If there are bad officers out there, how else would they be weeded out if no one goes through the proper channels to expose them?

CRIMINAL PROCEDURES

Without knowing where to look, taking classes in Criminal Justice, or working with or in the legal or law enforcement fields, the majority of citizens will not know or understand how officers are allowed to operate within the letter of the law including what powers and/or authorities they are given. *(None of this information is secret or hidden, and all of this information is public knowledge.)*

THE BILL OF RIGHTS

First, one needs to understand the Bill of Rights which are the First Ten Amendments of the Constitution. These amendments were written to protect individuals and prohibit the government from abusing its power. An overview of the Bill of Rights is as follows:

I. Freedom of religion, speech, press, assembly (peaceful protest), and petition
II. Right to bear arms
III. Quartering of troops
IV. Unreasonable searches and seizures
V. Grand Jury, double jeopardy, self-incrimination (right to remain silent), due process
VI. Criminal prosecution, right to a speedy and public trial, right to confront witnesses and counsel
VII. Common law suits
VIII. Excessive bail, excessive fines, cruel and unusual punishment
IX. Enumeration of certain rights (there are other rights for citizens that are not numbered in the amendments but are in the Constitution)
X. Rights reserved to the states and to the people

The amendment that predominantly comes into play during interaction between police and citizens is the 4th Amendment. It states, "*The right of the people to be secure in their persons, houses, papers, and effects, against unreasonable searches and seizures, shall not be violated, and no warrants shall issue, but upon probable cause, supported by oath or affirmation, and particularly describing the place to be searched, and the persons or things to be seized."*

ARTICULABLE REASONABLE SUSPICION AND PROBABLE CAUSE

In order for law enforcement to search or seize any person or property there has to be Articulable Reasonable Suspicion (ARS) and/or Probable Cause (PC).

- **Reasonable suspicion** is a reasonable presumption that a crime has been, is being, or will be committed. It is a reasonable belief based on facts or circumstances and is informed by a police officer's training and experience. Reasonable suspicion is seen as more than a guess or hunch but less than probable cause.
- **Probable cause** is the logical belief, **supported by facts and circumstances**, that a crime has been, is being, or will be committed.

The difference between the two terms is that probable cause means there is concrete evidence that a crime has been, is being, or will be committed, whereas reasonable suspicion is open to broader interpretation. Reasonable suspicion indicates that it *appears* as though a crime has been committed. The phrase is often used to justify investigation into suspicious behavior when a crime may have been committed. (Taylor Law Company)

For example: ARS – seeing a known drug dealer standing in front of a gas station. He or she has not done anything, but because of his or her prior history and not patronizing the business, the behavior can be viewed as suspicious. PC – watching this same known drug dealer conduct a hand-to-hand drug deal with several random people and vehicles in front of the business.

Everything a law enforcement officer does "must" have a lawful reason behind it. If a citizen is stopped by an officer, **he or she has the right to know why that officer is stopping him or her.** He or she also has the right to know the officer's name, badge number, and organization the officer represents. During a lawful investigation, if the officer who initiates the interaction does not voluntarily give up his or her information, the person stopped should get as much information as possible and he or she can file a complaint on the officer.

PAY ATTENTION!

There are different ways to obtain information from officers if the information is not volunteered. Some of the information that can be obtained without asking is:

Organization name - Look for patches on the officer's uniform or name of organization on patrol vehicle. It is also good to know the location of the interaction in order to determine what agency has jurisdiction in that area.

Officers' names - Look for a name tag and/or listen for the names of the officers if there is one or more officer present. If they talk to each other, try to listen to see what they call each other. If an officer does not give a name or have on a name tag, try to listen for his or her call sign over the radio. Every officer has a call sign or some type of identifier that is used over the radio. For example, I am Sergeant Jackson, but on the radio the call sign I respond to 2612 which is assigned to me for the purpose of radio traffic. So instead of the radio operator asking me, "Sergeant Jackson, are you ok? He or she would ask, "2612 are you ok?" Over the radio, 2612 is my name.

Officer description - Get a good look at the officer. Just like we, as officers, have to give out descriptions of suspects, get a good description of the officer. Height, weight, ethnicity, facial hair, hair color, eye color, and tattoos. These are some descriptors that can help identify which officer was interacting with you.

Date, Time, & Location - This is very important. Make sure you know the time and date of the interaction. Every "lawful" police interaction is recorded over the radio. To my understanding, most police vehicles have GPS. If an unlawful interaction occurs, try to remember the date, time, and location. This information can be used to pinpoint which officers were in that area at that time. An agency can also narrow down who was on duty at the time of the interaction.

IMPORTANT NOTICE

Due to the nature of some of the information an officer may receive prior to the interaction, the officer may not automatically give the reason for the stop for safety reasons, but the officer must give his or her name and organization represented when initiating contact with an individual.

Think about a traffic stop. An officer runs a tag and the information returned shows that the registered owner has a warrant. The officer can stop the vehicle and when making contact with the owner, if the owner is the driver, may not tell him or her right away the reason for the stop. The officer may ask for the driver's license, for verification purposes, and advise the owner/driver that the reason for the stop will be given momentarily. This gives the officer time to verify the identity and then strategize on how to get the person out of the vehicle, without incident and without alarming the owner/driver of the situation. Early notification to the driver that he or she has a warrant could give him or her the opportunity to flee and cause a situation that could put both the officer and citizen in danger. If the officer tells the person immediately that he or she has a warrant the likelihood of the person fleeing increases greatly which could lead to a use of force situation.

If a person is a suspect in an investigation, at the minimum, he or she has to surrender his or her state issued identification. If the identification is not available, he or she must give his or her full legal name and date of birth for verification purposes. Just like the officer has minimum information that he or she has to give, a person under investigation has to do the same. If an individual refuses to cooperate with officers during a lawful investigation, he or she can be charged with obstruction.

O.C.G.A.16-10-24. Obstructing or hindering law enforcement officers- (a) Except as otherwise provided in subsection (b) of this Code section, a person who knowingly and willfully obstructs or hinders any law enforcement officer in the lawful discharge of his official duties is guilty of a misdemeanor. (b) Whoever knowingly and willfully resists, obstructs, or opposes any law enforcement officer, prison guard, correctional officer, probation supervisor, parole supervisor, or conservation ranger in the lawful discharge of his official duties by offering or doing violence to the person of such officer or legally authorized person is guilty of a felony and shall, upon conviction thereof, be punished by imprisonment for not less than one nor more than five years.

In the case of traffic stops the law states:

O.C.G.A. 40-5-29. License to be carried and exhibited on demand (a) Every licensee shall have his driver's license in his immediate possession at all times when operating a motor vehicle. (b) Every licensee shall display his license upon the demand of a law enforcement officer. A refusal to comply with such demand not only shall constitute a violation of this subsection but shall also give rise to a presumption of a violation of subsection (a) of this Code section and of Code Section 40-5-20.

In the event that a person does not want to surrender his or her license and gives the officer a false name and date of birth, the law states:

O.C.G.A. 16-10-25. Giving false name, address, or birthdate to law enforcement officer - A person who gives a false name, address, or date of birth to a law enforcement officer in the lawful discharge of his official duties with the intent of misleading the officer as to his identity or birthdate is guilty of a misdemeanor.

So, in situations where an individual is the subject of an investigation, he or she has to surrender either his or her state issued identification, or give the officer his or her legal first name, last name, date of birth, and state the identification was issued in. Not shortened names, nicknames, or any other alias that the person goes by. It must be the name on his or her state issued license and/or identification card, and must be spelled the same way.

If an officer wants to just talk to an individual, called citizen contact, the individual has the right to refuse that interaction and go about his or her way. That person is not a suspect in an investigation.

Examples:

Probable Cause: Officer sees a vehicle weaving from one lane to another without signaling. The maneuvers of that vehicle are not that of a normal driver. The movements could be considered suspicious and give probable cause for the officer to initiate interaction with the driver.

Articulable Reasonable Suspicion: An individual is in an area known for high drug activity. The individual continuously looks at the officers, then peeks around a corner. This person's activity can be seen as not normal and suspicious.

Citizen Contact: a) Officer is on foot patrol in a shopping center. Contacts a passerby and says, "I'm Sergeant Jackson with the City of Morrow Police Department. Do you have a minute to talk about safety in the community?" Passerby answers, "No," and keeps walking.

b) Police at a high school for a presentation, student walks by and says "F*ck 12." Although disrespectful, it is not a crime and is not suspicious to a point of initiating an investigation.

SEARCH AND SEIZURE

There are several ways a search can be conducted. The most common one with police interaction is a warrantless search on a traffic stop or when an officer is using Probable Cause on a call. The following is a list of ways an officer is authorized to conduct a search without having to have a warrant:

a) **Consent.** Giving voluntary permission, by the individual being investigated, to an officer to search an area. The consent must be given free of coercion. At any given time during a consensual search, the person who consented can stop the search by verbally informing the officers that he or she no longer wants the search to continue.

b) **Plain View.** When an officer observes evidence to the case or evidence that is considered illegal, that is in the plain line of sight of said officer without the manipulation of any items to uncover said evidence.

Example: Officer arrives at a traffic accident. While checking for injuries on the parties involved, the officer observes a small bag of marijuana on the floor board of the driver's side of the vehicle. The officer did not move any items to uncover the marijuana and did not search the vehicle for it. The marijuana was in the plain line of sight of the officer while he was checking on the parties involved in the accident.

c) **Search incident to arrest.** When arresting an individual, the officer can search the individual for weapons and/or any items pertaining to the arrest.

Example: A person is pulled over for driving on a suspended license. When stopped, there is a strong odor of marijuana coming from the vehicle. The person is arrested and the person and vehicle can be searched for marijuana based on the smell coming from the vehicle.

Example: A person is pulled over for a suspended license. There is no smell of marijuana or any evidence of any other crime committed. Once the person is arrested, that is the end of the investigation. The officer has no probable cause to search the vehicle for any other reason. If the vehicle is being taken to impound, the officer can conduct a **vehicle inventory.**

d) **Vehicle Inventory.** An officer can inventory the contents of a vehicle to make sure that all property in the vehicle is listed on an inventory sheet and that all property will be returned to the owner once the vehicle is recovered from the impound yard. If something is discovered during an inventory, it can be used to file additional charges against the owner/operator and or occupants of the vehicle.

e) **Exigent Circumstances.** In a situation where officers feel as if evidence will be destroyed, or there is eminent danger to the officers or others present, police do not need a search warrant.

Example: Officers are dispatched to a suspicious person call at an abandoned house known for drug activity. Upon arrival at the location, officers see an individual outside. When the individual sees the officers he runs into the house and yells, "Get rid of it!"

Example: Officers get a call of a domestic assault in progress. When the officers arrive on scene they hear a person screaming for help. Due to the eminent danger and the nature of the call, the officers do not need a warrant to breach the location and locate the parties involved.

f) **Hot Pursuit.** If officers are actively in pursuit of a suspect and that suspect enters a private residence, the officers do not need a warrant to search the premises for the suspect. The scope of the search is also limited to the crime that has been committed.

   Example: If the suspect is an armed robbery suspect, still has the firearm on his or her person, and runs into a residence during a chase, the residence can be checked for the person and weapon.

   Example: If the suspect is a car theft suspect, abandons the vehicle and flees on foot into a residence, the residence can be searched for the suspect.

In all of these situations, excluding the inventory, the scope of the search is limited to what the officers are searching for. Remember the Fourth Amendment references "unreasonable" searches and seizures. So, if police are looking for a male 5' 10", 175 pounds who fled on foot to a residence, it would be reasonable to check closets, under beds, and crawlspaces. It would not be reasonable to check kitchen drawers, backpacks, and under dressers because those are not places a person that size can hide.

So according to the Constitution, law enforcement officers are given certain authorities to carry out their duties. At the same time, the Constitution protects citizens from officers who perform certain acts outside of the color of law. The main tool officers have that separates them from the citizens is the information under which they operate.

I implore you, as the reader, to educate yourself on common practices and procedures of law enforcement officers to better understand how officers operate and to protect yourself from possible confrontational and harmful situations.

5 DOMESTIC/ FAMILY VIOLENCE

Other than traffic stops, domestic violence is probably the most dangerous type of call a police officer will encounter. Domestic Violence is also defined as Family Violence according to the law. These situations are usually created and driven by a combination of quick reactions caused by an accelerated emotional state of mind. The victim and/or suspect is either physically, mentally, or emotionally hurt, or a combination of the three, which causes the victim or suspect to act erratically, leading to someone contacting law enforcement. In many domestic cases, calls to the police sometimes come from a third party, which is a person who is not directly involved, but hears or sees what is going on. Typical third party callers are children in the household, other family members, and neighbors.

In my experience, most domestic confrontations occur from a few variables; someone is hurt and wants the other party to feel the pain he or she is feeling, or one party is trying to control the other person, either by physical, mental, or emotional force.

WHAT IS CONSIDERED A DOMESTIC?

In the State of Georgia, there are three circumstances that determine if a relationship is domestic:

1. Relationships – married, blood related (siblings, mother vs. son, etc.)

2. If the two parties have children together

3. If the parties live or have lived together in the same household.

Most domestic situations are coupled with assaults or some type of property damage; that does not limit the scope of the situation. Domestics are handled differently in the courts. **Once a charge has been made in a domestic/family violence situation and an individual is arrested, only the courts can rescind the charges.** When there is a situation like a fight or an assault between parties that does not fall under the Family Violence Statute, the victim can choose to press charges if he or she wants. That choice is not an option in domestics. In domestic cases the state prosecutes the accused.

O.C.G.A. 19-13-1. "Family violence" defined: As used in this article, the term "family violence" means the occurrence of one or more of the following acts between past or present spouses, persons who are parents of the same child, parents and children, stepparents and stepchildren, foster parents and foster children, or other persons living or formerly living in the same household: (1) ***Any felony****; or (2) Commission of offenses of battery, simple battery, simple assault, assault, stalking, criminal damage to property, unlawful restraint, or criminal trespass.*

SIDE NOTE

POLICE SHOULD NEVER BE CALLED OR USED TO TRY AND SCARE ANOTHER PARTY.

Police officers are **law enforcement.** Even though one party's intention may not be to have the other party arrested, if a crime has been committed, depending on the severity of the offense, the officer must act according to the crime that is being reported and evidence presented. Therefore, for anyone who is acting out of a heightened emotional state, he or she should calm down, think about what he or she truly wants to do in this confrontational situation, then act accordingly. Once the police show up, if there is sufficient evidence to validate that a crime has taken place, the victim no longer has the authority to choose what happens.

SCENARIOS

The following are some examples of common domestic situations that officers may encounter:

Scenario 1

Wife is upset with Husband because she found pictures and messages from another woman in his phone. They get into a verbal dispute. Wife is trying to take Husband's phone. In the process of her trying to take his phone, she jumps on his back, hits him in the head, and scratches his arms and hands. Husband responds by pushing Wife to the floor to separate himself from her. Wife calls the police claiming he should not have put his hands on her and she wants him arrested.

When police show up, they conduct their investigation. In my experience, based on what is given in this example, Wife would be considered the primary aggressor due to the fact that she initiated the physical contact and the Husband has visible injuries. The Husband acted in self-defense and was trying to get her off of him. At this point the wife would be faced with being charged with Family Violence Battery. Now if Husband pushes Wife on the ground, then picks up a chair and hits her with it or punches her in the face repeatedly knocking her unconscious, he now becomes the primary aggressor based on an excessive act of force after separating himself from Wife.

A lot of what is determined is based on the information given to the officers. If there are no visible injuries and the parties are unwilling to be forthcoming with the information needed to make certain prosecutorial actions, officers can only investigate to the extent of what is given. Other factors that can come into consideration are a known history between the parties and non-corroborative witnesses (a witness who can give a neutral account of an incident not in favor of either party). **Just because a person calls the police does not automatically mean that he or she is right in the situation.** A determination will be made based on the evidence at the scene and testimonies of the event.

Scenario 2

Parent is in a verbal dispute with Child. Parent is tired of being disrespected by Child. There is no physical contact and no threats made. Child curses Parent out on a consistent basis and refuses to abide by instructions given from the parent. Child does not want to follow any house rules. Child gets angry and locks his/herself in a room and tells Parent to stay the F#@k away from him or her. Parent calls police to scare Child about his or her behavior.

In this example, no crime has been committed so police officers are very limited in what they can do. An officer can talk to the child, but if the parent has been dealing with this child for the amount of years that the child is old, what does the parent feasibly believe the officer can do in the limited time the officer is on the scene? In my opinion, I feel like in cases like this, parents weaken their power base by calling police about disrespectful behavior. Yes, it is disrespectful, but disrespect is not a crime. Police are **"law enforcement"** and if no laws have been broken, then there is nothing an officer can enforce. The child sees the parent calling the police, the police do what's possible in a limited capacity, and the child views the call as an empty threat. Now the child thinks he or she can do whatever he or she wants and even the police cannot stop him or her. This puts the child in a power position and it appears to the child that he or she is the superior entity in the household.

Under GA Code 16-5-23.1 Battery Section F Subsection 2 it states:

O.C.G.A 16-5-23.1 (f) If the offense of battery is committed between past or present spouses, persons who are parents of the same child, parents and children, stepparents and stepchildren, foster parents and foster children, or other persons living or formerly living in the same household, then such offense shall constitute the offense of family violence battery and shall be punished as follows: (2) Upon a second or subsequent conviction of family violence battery against the same or another victim, the defendant shall be guilty of a felony and shall be punished by imprisonment for not less than one, nor more than five years. ***In no event shall this subsection be applicable to "reasonable" corporal punishment administered by parent to child.***

Now, what is considered reasonable corporal punishment? That is a gray area parents need to figure out, because there is a ***very, very*** fine line between punishment and abuse as may be interpreted in the eyes of the law. Parents and guardians, you have to know how far you can go when implementing physical discipline to the children under your care. Unfortunately, there is no clear-cut guideline.

Scenario 3

Friend 1 and friend 2 have a conversation. Friend 2 has fallen on hard financial times and needs help with a place to stay. Friend 1 extends a helping hand and tells Friend 2 that he or she can stay at Friend 1's residence until Friend 2 gets financially stable. There is no written contract and everything has been agreed on verbally because "friends don't do friends dirty." Six weeks go by and Friend 1 is fed up with the way Friend 2 keeps his or her area clean. Friend 1 is upset because Friend 2 has different people coming over to visit and spend the night all of the time. Friend 1 has discovered that some of his or her property has been used and mishandled, plus Friend 2 has only paid half of the agreed upon rent for the first month. Friend 1, not being knowledgeable of the landlord/tenant guidelines, calls the police and says, "I want friend 2 out of here today." Friend 2 advises he or she is not going anywhere and Friend 1 has to have him or her evicted. Even though the situation has the possibility to escalate into a worse situation, Friend 2 is correct.

RESIDENCY

At this point the situation is a civil matter between roommates. It is considered domestic, for reporting purposes, because the parties live together, but in this scenario no crime has been committed. If a crime has not been committed, police can suggest and ask Friend 2 if he or she *voluntarily* wants to leave because of the unrest at the residence. However, police cannot force anyone to leave if residency has been established by both parties. According to the Georgia Landlord-Tenant Handbook, it states:

Written vs. verbal lease*. A written lease provides certainty and clarity and helps resolve disputes. For example, a tenant should make sure the rent amount is clear and cannot be increased during the lease term. Verbal leases often lead to misunderstandings about what was agreed upon. A tenant who occupies property and pays rent without a written lease is a "tenant-at-will" and certain laws such as those regarding eviction and security deposits still apply. A landlord must give a sixty (60) day notice to terminate or increase rent and the tenant must give a thirty (30) day notice to terminate or change the agreement. It is best to put the notice in writing. If the tenant fails to pay rent, the landlord can immediately demand possession and file a* ***dispossessory affidavit.***

In my personal opinion, if a person has a primary residence by his or herself, not two people going in on a lease together and moving in at the same time, unless you are getting married and you are a husband and wife moving in together, **DO NOT** take on a roommate if you do not have to. In my experience, if things go bad, they usually go really bad. This includes, boyfriends and girlfriends, boyfriends and boyfriends, girlfriends and girlfriends, parents and adult children, adult relatives, classmates, friends, etc. Adults have a hard time living under another adult's rules. When those different lifestyles clash, it usually never ends favorably for either party.

If a roommate is taken on, make sure a lease or written contract is done and all the stipulations are outlined, just like in a rental agreement with an apartment or house. Make sure it's outlined what happens if someone violates the lease and know the eviction process. This way there are no surprises if someone has to be evicted.

O.C.G.A 19-2-1. Place of domicile; how domicile changed, generally: (a) The domicile of every person who is of full age and is laboring under no disability is the place where the family of the person permanently resides, if in this state. If a person has no family or if his family does not reside in this state, the place where the person generally lodges shall be considered his domicile.

In the roommate's section of the Georgia Landlord-Tenant Handbook it states:

Roommates. *Individuals who plan to rent a unit with a roommate(s) should be aware of the following:*

- *Each roommate who is in a tenant relationship with the landlord can be held responsible for the full amount of the rent due. For example, if all the roommates sign the lease and one moves out, the others will be responsible for the full rent. However, if you end up paying more than your share of the rent, you can sue your former roommate to recover the difference in civil court.*

- *Landlords collect money from tenants who actually signed the lease agreement. Roommates who did not sign the lease are not legally liable to the landlord unless the landlord accepted payment from the roommate or other actions established a landlord-tenant relationship.*

• *Security deposits are usually divided equally among the tenants. Landlords should try to spell out the terms of the security deposit in the lease's terms.*

• *Landlords do not have legal means to step in and resolve roommate disputes unless there is a lease violation or criminal act.*

TEMPORARY PROTECTION

Domestic encounters are taken very seriously by police and the courts. One reason is because of the close proximity in which the parties are to each other. Judges can mandate stay away or no violent contact orders to try to keep individuals from repeating the behavior that landed them in the legal system. Individuals can file Temporary Protection Orders (TPO) also known as restraining orders by going to the courts and filing a petition. At all costs, regardless of the situation, if an individual is court ordered to stay away from another person, **STAY AWAY!**

I have conducted investigations where a male and female got into a dispute and the male was court ordered to stay a certain distance from the female. Both parties were served with the proper paperwork. Let's say the order stated the male had to stay away from the female for six months. Tension dies down and they are in their third month of the order. The female invites the male over to talk. The male goes to the residence to talk. There has been no aggression between the two for three months so he feels as if it is ok. He gets to the house and they talk, have dinner, and become intimate. Well, she starts to think about the things he did three months ago that led to the current situation and she gets emotional and upset. They get into an argument and she calls the police and says he is not supposed to be there and she has paperwork. The police show up and find the two parties together. The police are given the paperwork signed by both parties through a court that states the male is not supposed to be around her for another three months. The male is arrested for violating the TPO. He argues she invited him over and all sorts of activities took place while he was there. He explains she got mad after thinking about the situation, then called the police on him.

Once again, people have to understand that police are "law enforcement." Based on the evidence given when police arrive, the documents signed by a judge and both parties advising the situation and the stipulations in which that situation has to be lawfully enforced, the male is at fault. The male has no argument at that time because he knew he was supposed to stay away from the female for that allotted time. If a judge issues an order like described, do not violate the statutes in that order for any reason because one never knows how the other party can or will use it against them.

Another situation that I have witnessed: Male met Female who is a single mother of three children, has fallen on some hard times and needs a place to stay. Male allowed Female and her children to move into the bottom level of his split-level home that he paid for and owns. Female had been there for a few months. Female claimed that Male made several sexual advances toward her. Female advised she continuously refused the advances. Female advised that Male started to get more and more aggressive the more she refused. Female claimed that Male got angry due to the constant rejection which caused her to fear for her safety. Female filed a Temporary Protection Order against Male.

I arrived on scene with several sheriffs to serve Male with the Temporary Protection Order. The court date on the order is scheduled for 3-4 months from the day served. Male was given enough time to gather whatever personal belongings he would need to get by for a few months and was ordered not to return to his house until after the court date and the judge makes a ruling.

This was a very unfortunate situation for the male, but because he allowed the female to establish residency, she had the same rights to the residence as he did, regardless of ownership.

REVENGE PORN

This section addresses a fairly new issue that has started occurring with the advancement in technology called, prohibition on nude or sexually explicit electronic transmissions. This law outlines the issue of former lovers using personal nude photos, videos, or other media against one another. The photos would have been taken consensually between two adults during their relationship without ill will. After breaking up, one or both of the parties threaten to use the photos as a way to get back at the other by sending them to loved ones, co-workers, bosses, or posting them on social media, etc. Although this method has been used by teens and adolescents, the charges are different because the individuals are under age (See the Chapter for Teens). The following law outlines the definitions of this charge:

O.C.G.A 16-11-90 - Prohibition on nude or sexually explicit electronic transmissions- (a) As used in this Code section, the term: (1) "Harassment" means engaging in conduct directed at a depicted person that is intended to cause substantial emotional harm to the depicted person.(2) "Nudity" means: (A) The showing of the human male or female genitals, pubic area, or buttocks without any covering or with less than a full opaque covering; (B) The showing of the female breasts without any covering or with less than a full opaque covering; or (C) The depiction of covered male genitals in a discernibly turgid state. (3) "Sexually explicit conduct" shall have the same meaning as set forth in Code Section 16-12-100.

(b) A person violates this Code section if he or she, knowing the content of a transmission or post, knowingly and without the consent of the depicted person: (1) Electronically transmits or posts, in one or more transmissions or posts, a photograph or video which depicts nudity or sexually explicit conduct of an adult when the transmission or post is harassment or causes financial

loss to the depicted person and serves no legitimate purpose to the depicted person; or (2) Causes the electronic transmission or posting, in one or more transmissions or posts, of a photograph or video which depicts nudity or sexually explicit conduct of an adult when the transmission or post is harassment or causes financial loss to the depicted person and serves no legitimate purpose to the depicted person.

(c) Any person who violates this Code section shall be guilty of a misdemeanor of a high and aggravated nature; provided, however, that upon a second or subsequent violation of this Code section, he or she shall be guilty of a felony and, upon conviction thereof, shall be punished by imprisonment of not less than one nor more than five years, a fine of not more than $100,000.00, or both.

(d) A person shall be subject to prosecution in this state pursuant to Code Section 17-2-1 for any conduct made unlawful by this Code section which the person engages in while: (1) Either within or outside of this state if, by such conduct, the person commits a violation of this Code section which involves an individual who resides in this state; or (2) Within this state if, by such conduct, the person commits a violation of this Code section which involves an individual who resides within or outside this state.

(e) The provisions of subsection (b) of this Code section shall not apply to: (1) The activities of law enforcement and prosecution agencies in the investigation and prosecution of criminal offenses; (2) Legitimate medical, scientific, or educational activities; (3) Any person who transmits or posts a photograph or video depicting only himself or

herself engaged in nudity or sexually explicit conduct; (4) The transmission or posting of a photograph or video that was originally made for commercial purposes; or (5) Any person who transmits or posts a photograph or video depicting a person voluntarily engaged in nudity or sexually explicit conduct in a public setting; or (6) The transmission is made pursuant to or in anticipation of a civil action.

(f) There shall be a rebuttable presumption that an information service, system, or access software provider that provides or enables computer access by multiple users to a computer server, including specifically a service or system that provides access to the Internet, for content provided by another person, does not know the content of an electronic transmission or post.

(g) Any violation of this Code section shall constitute a separate offense and shall not merge with any other crimes set forth in this title.

IF YOU ARE WITH SOMEONE WHO CALLS THE POLICE ON YOU OR YOU FEEL YOU NEED TO CALL THE POLICE ON, YOU MAY WANT TO RETHINK WHO YOU ARE WITH!!

THINK LONG AND HARD ABOUT WHO YOU ALLOW IN YOUR HOUSEHOLD, YOUR MOTIVATION BEHIND THE REASON FOR ALLOWING THEM TO STAY, AND IF IT IS WORTH THE NEGATIVE RESULTS IF THE SITUATION GOES BAD!

6 TRAFFIC

First things first! By law, when pulled over the driver is supposed to pull to the right of the road. If there is a curb, make sure it is safe to pull over and stop as close to the curb as possible and clear of all intersections. The driver can pull into a parking lot or onto a side street, but always try to stop on the right side of the road. Do not stop in center turning lanes or intersections; if at all possible do not make a left turn across oncoming traffic to pull into a parking lot.

O.C.G.A. 40-6-74. Operation of vehicles on approach of authorized emergency vehicles: (a) Upon the immediate approach of an authorized emergency vehicle or a vehicle belonging to a federal, state, or local law enforcement agency making use of an audible signal and visual signals meeting the requirements of Code Section 40-6-6, the driver of every other vehicle shall yield the right of way and shall immediately drive to a position parallel to, and as close as possible to, the right-hand edge or curb of the roadway clear of any intersection and shall stop and remain in such position until the authorized emergency vehicle or law enforcement vehicle has passed, except when otherwise directed by a police officer.

CITATIONS/TICKETS

A CITATION IS A TICKET!!! If the officer says to a driver/owner of a vehicle, "I am writing you a citation for …" **this means the driver/owner of the vehicle is getting a ticket**. Pay attention to the contact information for the court and pay ***special*** attention to the court date. If the driver/owner wants to take care of the citation without going to court, he or she can call the court for further information. If the driver/owner does not take care of the citation prior to the court date, GO TO COURT! Once a signature is on that citation, there is no excuse. The, "Nobody told me", "I didn't get anything in the mail", or "I did not know" will not suffice as a valid excuse for not taking care of the citation or showing up to court. A judge will issue a bench warrant for the responsible party's arrest for FAILURE TO APPEAR if the offender does not appear in court. The signature means it is the responsibility of the person issued the citation to either go to court and/or take care of the violation. If the citation is a warning, then that's exactly what it is, a warning; no court date or fine.

A ticket is not an admission of guilt, and all persons signing one should be informed of this by the issuing officer. A ticket is the written acknowledgement stating that the offender understands that the officer is claiming to have observed the violation on the citation committed with his or her trained eyes. The person issued the violation has the right to go to court and show his or burden of proof that he or she did not commit the crime alleged. That responsibility is on the offender. The majority of traffic infractions, in today's police culture, are recorded. It is the responsibility of the accused to secure the video if he or she wants to use it as evidence to disprove the charge.

WHAT IS A CRIME?

Crime is defined as an action or omission that constitutes an offense that may be prosecuted by the state and is punishable by law, illegal activities, an illegal act for which someone can be punished by the government; *especially*: a gross violation of law (Merriam-Webster).

O.C.G.A. 16-2-1. "Crime" defined: (a) A "crime" is a violation of a statute of this state in which there is a joint operation of an act or omission to act and intention or criminal negligence. (b) Criminal negligence is an act or failure to act which demonstrates a willful, wanton, or reckless disregard for the safety of others who might reasonably be expected to be injured thereby.

By law, there are only two types of crimes: a felony and a misdemeanor. The difference between the two is the amount of time an individual will serve in confinement if convicted. A misdemeanor is a crime punishable by less than one year. A felony is a crime that is punishable by one year or more, up to a life sentence.

So why is it that so many people believe that they have not committed a crime when it comes to traffic offenses?

Under Title 40 it states: Enacted in 1974, the Uniform Rules of the Road regulate behavior on the state's roads. Various sections prescribe the rules concerning, for example, traffic signs; right of way; rights and duties of pedestrians; turning, starting, and signaling; speed restrictions; and stopping, standing, and parking. *Except for sections which provide <u>some other specific punishment</u>,* ***a violation defined in any provision of the Uniform Rules of the Road is a "MISDEMEANOR".*** (Georgia Law Enforcement Handbook 2014-15)

So, to clear up this myth, all traffic offenses are misdemeanor crimes. Exceptions are ones that provide a specific punishment for certain traffic offenses like, vehicular homicide or serious injury by motor vehicle, which are felonies. So, when a person is pulled over and the officer advises him or her the reason he or she got pulled over, understand that the officer is advising him or her that a crime, according to Georgia Law, was observed. No matter how petty he or she may think it is, by the book a crime is a crime.

Title 40 in the Georgia Law Enforcement Handbook is the section that covers Motor Vehicles and Traffic. Chapter 1 covers General Provisions which include definitions such as alcohol concentration, what is a bus, who is a driver, what is a motor vehicle, and other definitions of subjects that pertain to motor vehicles and traffic.

Chapter 2 is the chapter that most people deal with when it comes to getting pulled over and receiving citations. To reiterate, 40-2-2 states, *except as otherwise provided in this chapter, any person who violates any provision of this chapter shall be guilty of a* ***misdemeanor.*** I emphasize this because as an officer I am told quite often, "Y'all need to be out there fighting real crime", "I did not commit a crime", "This is not even a misdemeanor", "This doesn't make any sense", "There are people out here committing real crimes", and "You're just making up stuff," amongst other comments due to a lack of knowing or understanding the law.

Police, sheriffs, state patrols, and deputies are law enforcement. Their jobs are to enforce the laws. This includes all of the laws. There is such a thing as officer discretion which, gives an officer an amount of leeway as to how he or she can handle certain violations. The same way a judge can use leniency in the court house, officers can "choose" to handle **certain** violations a certain way. It is our choice on a case-by-case basis, not a right to anyone including fellow law enforcement personnel.

For example, take driving with no license 40-5-20 and driving while a license suspended or revoked 40-5-121. As stated earlier, all violations are misdemeanors except ones that are specified by the law to be felonies. In a situation like this, if I stop someone and they are driving on a suspended license, I can take the individual to jail or I can perform a cite-and-release, based on the situation. This means I can give the person a citation and release them to another legally licensed person. I usually give the individual the opportunity to contact a licensed driver, or if there is a licensed driver in the vehicle with the individual, I verify the other person's license, cite the original driver, and release them. This is an example of exercising officer discretion.

A situation where this may occur is when the driver is a 35-year-old parent and he or she has two small children in the vehicle. The passenger is a 19-year-old co-worker with a valid license. I would cite the driver and release the individual on the grounds that the 19-year-old cannot take custody of the driver's two children. Again, this is using discretion, each officer could respond differently and in this scenario are not obligated to handle it in this manner.

A few violations that people think are not crimes:

- 40-8-23 – Taillights and Tag Lights
- 40-8-74 – Tire Requirements
- 40-8-22 – Headlights
- 40-2-8 – Expired Registration, Improper Placement of Revalidation Sticker, No County Decal on Tag, Operating without a valid tag

- 40-5-29 – License not on person, License to be carried and exhibited on demand
- 40-5-20 – New Resident to obtain license within 30 days
- 40-6-251 – Laying drag (spinning out tires)
- 40-6-74 – Pulling over to the left instead of pulling over to the right when pulled over or approached by emergency vehicles.

These and hundreds of other violations under Title 40 as stated above are all misdemeanor crimes. I encourage you to research these laws and others to make sure you know that you are in the right before confronting an officer about your perception of what you believe the law is. Know that law enforcement officers are required to know the laws they are enforcing, and if there is a law in question, the officer will know where to get the information in order to clarify his or her decision.

REFUSING TO SIGN A TICKET

"So, what happens if I refuse to sign a ticket?"

I'm glad you asked.

O.C.G.A 40-13-2.1. Signature on citations required; effect of failure to sign: (a) A person who is issued a citation as provided in this chapter or Code Section 17-6-11, relating to display of driver's license in lieu of bail, ***shall sign the citation to acknowledge receipt of the citation and of his***

or her obligation to appear for trial. *The officer shall advise the person that signing the citation is not an admission of guilt and that* ***failure to sign will result in the person having to post a cash bond.*** *If the person* ***refuses to sign the citation, it shall constitute reasonable cause to believe that the person will not appear at trial and the officer may bring the person before a judicial officer or traffic violations bureau to post a bond as is otherwise provided by law.***

Question: "How can an officer make sure that a person who refuses to sign a ticket, appears before a judicial officer and pays the cash bond?"

Answer: **By taking the person to JAIL.**

Before signing a ticket or citation, I encourage anyone who is given one to read the notice above your signature line. It states:

This citation shall constitute official notice to you that failure to appear in Court at the date and time stated on this citation to dispose of the cited charges against you shall cause the designated Court to forward your driver's license number to the Department of Driver Services, and your driver's license shall be suspended. (Georgia Code 17-6-11 and 40-5-56) The suspension shall remain in effect until such time as there is a satisfactory disposition in this matter or the Court notifies the Department of Driver Services.

In other words, don't just take a ticket, ball it up and throw it away because you are upset. There is an opportunity to dispute the citation in court on the date given. Don't dismiss it and think if you ignore it, it will go away. Oh, and one of my favorites, "I didn't get anything in the mail." By the way, if you go to court and say something like, "This is my old address I moved 4 months ago and I never changed my address." Guess what? 40-5-33, you can catch another charge for not changing your address within 60 days of relocating.

Bottom line, your signature on the citation is your notification. If you do not take care of the citation prior to the court date or show up in court, your license shall be suspended and you risk having a bench warrant taken out on you for Failure to Appear in court.

So when you know you signed the citation, did not go to court, and did not take care of the citation prior to the court date, do not fight and argue with the next officer who pulls you over and takes you to jail for Failure to Appear and/or driving while license suspended or revoked.

PASSENGERS (Recheck 4th Amendment)

I want to talk about passengers for a little bit. The best thing a passenger can do in certain situations during a traffic stop is BE QUIET! The traffic stop pertains to the driver or owner of the vehicle, the violation accused of: either moving, equipment, or licensing of the registered owner, and the vehicle. As a passenger, once you decide to interject during the officer's investigation, you have now become part of the investigation and are subject to further investigation. A passenger's interjection can cause further issues for a driver. It can cause an officer to look more closely at violations that may have been overlooked.

The traffic stop, as stated earlier, is about either the driver or registered owner, equipment violation, moving violation, and/or vehicle violation. Initially, the passenger has nothing to do with the stop unless the officer observes a violation by a passenger or the situation gives the officer probable cause to investigate the passenger. For example, the officer observes the passenger with no seatbelt in the front seat, an odor of marijuana in the vehicle, unusual movements by the passenger i.e. reaching into the back seat, reaching under the front seat, and acting nervous or suspicious, may all be reasons for a police officer to further investigate the passenger and parties in a vehicle.

If the registered owner is the passenger of the vehicle and the vehicle is stopped for a violation like no insurance or expired tag, even though the owner is not driving, he or she is still responsible for the vehicle and can receive a citation for the infraction.

If a situation occurs that gives the officer probable cause to investigate further, and the passenger refuses to cooperate, he or she can be charged with obstruction of justice:

O.C.G.A. 16-10-24 Obstructing or hindering a law enforcement officer: (a) Except as otherwise provided in subsection (b) of this Code section, a person who knowingly and willfully obstructs or hinders any law enforcement officer in the lawful discharge of his official duties is guilty of a misdemeanor. (b) Whoever knowingly and willfully resists, obstructs, or opposes any law enforcement officer, prison guard, correctional officer, probation supervisor, parole supervisor, or conservation ranger in the lawful discharge of his official duties by offering or doing violence to the person of such officer or legally authorized person is guilty of a felony and shall, upon conviction thereof, be punished by imprisonment for not less than one nor more than five years.

COMMON QUESTIONS

Why do so many cops show up for one car? Often times, officers show up to back another officer for safety purposes. Sometimes certain information is received through the computer system and alerts other officers that the situation warrants a heightened level of alert due to information discovered.

What do I do if I do *not* feel safe in an area that is secluded and away from the public? All "lawful" traffic stops are recorded through the dispatch radio system. The driver can call 9-1-1, give his or her location, vehicle description, and tag number and ask the 9-1-1 operator if there is an officer conducting a traffic stop in that area on their vehicle.

What should be done if there is a weapon in the vehicle? The driver can volunteer the information on the stop or an officer may ask if there is a weapon in the vehicle. First, keep your hands visible and tell the officer where the weapon is. In my experience one of two things will happen

if the weapon is within the reach of the driver: a) the officer will separate the driver from the vehicle and weapon by asking the driver to exit the vehicle and stay in an area where the officer can maintain visibility of the driver, or b) separate the weapon from the driver and the vehicle. The officer will ask the driver where the weapon is. After the driver advises the location, the officer will remove the weapon from the vehicle, make it safe, and continue his or her traffic stop.

In both of these situations, the driver should keep his or her hands on the steering wheel and should not make any sudden moves. Do not lie! If a driver says there are no weapons in the vehicle and, for example, the driver is arrested and a weapon is discovered when the driver is searched, this will put the officers on a very high alert and can escalate the situation.

How should I react when pulled over? Traffic stops can be very nerve-wrecking for many citizens. Many citizens do not realize an infraction has been committed, some may forget to update the vehicle registration, some may not realize the lapse of insurance has caused their registration to be suspended. Those are just a few situations that have caused officers to initiate traffic stops.

When pulled over, try to remain calm, cooperate with the officer, and try to maintain composure. Listen to what the officer is saying before reacting out of emotion.

What should the officer do upon approaching the vehicle? The officer should announce his or her name, say what agency he or she represents, advise the reason for the stop, and he or she can ask a question pertaining to the stop. For example: “I am Sergeant Jackson, with the City of Morrow Police Department. I stopped you because I observed you driving through a stop sign without stopping, is there any lawful reason why you did not stop?” This is just an example, but the verbal interaction should at a minimum contain this information.

As the driver, what should you do? Give the officer your driver’s license and/or vehicle registration and insurance information if requested. At the minimum the driver’s license is required. In the State of Georgia, it is required that every operator of a motor vehicle have the proper driver’s license for the type of vehicle he or she is operating. For drivers with restricted licenses, the operator must drive within the parameters of the restrictions. It is also Georgia Law that the driver must have his or her physical driver’s license on his or her person when operating a vehicle. If a driver does not have his or her driver’s license on his or her person, he or she must give the officer a correct name and date of birth and the state in which the valid license or identification was issued.

O.C.G.A 40-5-29. License to be carried and exhibited on demand: (a) Every licensee shall have his driver's license in his immediate possession at all times when operating a motor vehicle. (b) Every licensee shall display his license upon the demand of a law enforcement officer. A refusal to comply with such demand not only shall constitute a violation of this subsection but shall also give rise to a presumption of a violation of subsection (a) of this Code section and of Code Section 40-5-20.

BY ALL MEANS, DO NOT GIVE THE OFFICER A FALSE NAME AND/OR DATE OF BIRTH. Many people who know they do not have a license, have a suspended license, or think he or she has a warrant will sometimes give an officer a false name or date of birth trying to deter the officer from finding his or her correct information. This is a jailable offense and the person who gives the false information can be arrested.

O.C.G.A. 16-10-25. Giving false name, address, or birthdate to law enforcement officer: A person who gives a false name, address, or date of birth to a law enforcement officer in the lawful discharge of his official duties with the intent of misleading the officer as to his identity or birthdate is guilty of a misdemeanor.

What shouldn't you do? Argue while pulled over. Signing a citation does not admit guilt. It is your responsibility. If you do not agree with the officer's decision, the time to prove him or her wrong is in court, not on the side of the road. Being argumentative can escalate a situation unnecessarily and cause alarm for the officer. Once the court date is given, the offender needs to begin building his or her case to prove that they feel the officer's citation is incorrect. It is the offender's responsibility to prove the officer wrong IN COURT and NOT ON THE SIDE OF THE ROAD. Once again, a refusal to sign the citation will result in the offender going to jail.

OVERVIEW

I hope this chapter has helped you gain a better understanding of traffic laws and procedures during traffic stops (Also see Criminal Procedures). There are a lot of people responding to officers based on the hype and sensitization of police/citizen interactions on media and social media. There is a lot of misinformation being transmitted which causes people to react negatively. I implore everyone to research the offense by the code on the ticket, and be honest with his or herself about whether or not the violation was committed.

Pull over to the right side of road as safely as possible. Tell your passengers to be quiet. Unless there is a violation committed by a passenger, the majority of traffic stops have nothing to do with the passengers. Passengers can escalate a situation unnecessarily and cause more problems for the driver/owner of the vehicle.

If there is a weapon in the vehicle be honest and do not reach for it. Allow the officer to separate the weapon from your person or separate you from the weapon if in the vehicle. Most traffic stops are being recorded by the officer either via vehicle dashcam and/or body cameras. If you are going to record the interaction, do not allow that to be a distraction during the stop. There is no law that I know of prohibiting an interaction to be recorded. If an officer is conducting his or herself professionally and in a lawful manner, he or she should not have a problem being recorded.

Finally, the burden of proof is on you to disprove that the infraction was committed by you. Do not argue on the side of the road with the officer. Wait until you go to court. Pay attention to the court date and time; use the time in between to build your case. If you are going to just pay the fine then do that. If you are not going to pay or need time to pay, GO TO COURT! Do not ignore the court date and get a warrant issued for your arrest for failure to appear unnecessarily. All of the information needed to take care of the citation is on the copy issued.

TAKE CARE AND DRIVE SAFELY!

7 USE OF FORCE

A lot of people have questions as to why officers are allowed to use the type of force they see necessary in order to stop a threat or make an effective arrest. In my training, I have found that there are four primary laws in the State of Georgia that authorize the use of force.

The first one pertains only to those who are sworn law enforcement officers:

O.C.G.A. 17-4-20- Authorization of arrests with and without warrants generally; use of deadly force; adoption or promulgation of conflicting regulations, policies, ordinances, and resolutions; (b)- Sheriffs and peace officers who are appointed or employed in conformity with Chapter 8 of Title 35 may use deadly force to apprehend a suspected felon only when the officer reasonably believes ***that the suspect possesses a deadly weapon or any object,***

device, or instrument which, when used offensively against a person, *is likely to or actually does result in serious bodily injury;* *when the officer reasonably believes* ***that the suspect poses an immediate threat of physical violence to the officer or others;*** *or when there is probable cause to believe that the suspect has committed a crime involving the infliction or threatened infliction of serious physical harm.* *Nothing in this Code section shall be construed so as to restrict such sheriffs or peace officers from the use of such reasonable nondeadly force as may be necessary to apprehend and arrest a suspected felon or misdemeanant.*

This code section provides an explanation as to when officers are allowed to use deadly force. Officers are given more latitude when making that decision than the general public. The basis of this statute is the U.S. Supreme Court ruling on the case Graham vs. Connor. This case established the objective reasonableness standard that holds officers accountable when using force. It also established when an officer can use force and how much force can be used depending on the situation. There is no set standard for using force because each case is unique in its own circumstances. It is based on, whether or not a reasonable officer responds the same way as the officer in the use of force situation, if that officer was in the same predicament.

The second statute explains the justification laws based on if an officer claims that he or she used **reasonable force** in a given situation. It is as follows:

*<u>O.C.G.A. 16-3-20. Justification</u> - The fact that **a person's** conduct is justified is a defense to prosecution for any crime based on that conduct. The defense of justification can be claimed:(1) When the person's conduct is justified under Code Section 16-3-21, 16-3-23, 16-3-24, 16-3-25, or 16-3-26; (2) When the person's conduct is in reasonable fulfillment of his duties as a government officer or employee; (3) When the person's conduct is the reasonable discipline of a minor by his parent or a person in loco parentis; (4) When the person's conduct is reasonable and is performed in the course of making a lawful arrest; (5) When the person's conduct is justified for any other reason under the laws of this state; or (6) In all other instances which stand upon the same footing of reason and justice as those enumerated in this article.*

Subsection (2) justifies use of force for officers by stating "fulfillment of his duties as a government officer or employee. The rest of the subsections can pertain to anyone in the public who uses force in a given situation to protect self, property, or others.

*<u>O.C.G.A. 16-3-21. Use of force in defense of self or others</u>: (a) **<u>A person</u>** is justified in threatening or using force against another when and to the extent that he or she reasonably believes that <u>such threat or force is necessary to defend himself or herself or a third person against such other's imminent use o,f unlawful force</u>; however, except as provided in Code Section 16-3-23 (Use of force in defense of habitation) a person is justified in using force which is*

intended or likely to cause death or great bodily harm only if he or she reasonably believes that such force is necessary to prevent death or great bodily injury to himself or herself or a third person or to prevent the commission of a forcible felony.

(b) A person is not justified in using force under the circumstances specified in subsection (a) of this Code section if he:(1) Initially provokes the use of force against himself with the intent to use such force as an excuse to inflict bodily harm upon the assailant; (2) Is attempting to commit, committing, or fleeing after the commission or attempted commission of a felony; or (3) Was the aggressor or was engaged in a combat by agreement unless he withdraws from the encounter and effectively communicates to such other person his intent to do so and the other, notwithstanding, continues or threatens to continue the use of unlawful force.

(c) Any rule, regulation, or policy of any agency of the state or any ordinance, resolution, rule, regulation, or policy of any county, municipality, or other political subdivision of the state which is in conflict with this Code section shall be null, void, and of no force and effect.

What this basically states is that a person is justified in using force against another person to defend his or herself and to help protect others from unlawful force. For example, if a person is getting beat up by four people, those around can use the correct amount of force (pulling them off of the person, striking the attackers, etc.) in the defense of the person who is getting beat up. This could include the use of deadly force due to the fact that four people assaulting one person can kill that person.

It does not apply if someone initiates the assault for the purpose of hurting someone else, assaults someone to get away while committing a crime, or a situation where there is a fight between mutual parties. One person says, "Ok, I'm done," and tries to walk away, but the other person goes after him or her and assaults them (subsection (b).

O.C.G.A. 16-3-24.2 - Immunity from prosecution; exception - A person who uses threats or force in accordance with Code Section 16-3-21, 16-3-23, 16-3-23.1, or 16-3-24 shall be immune from criminal prosecution therefore unless in the use of deadly force, such person utilizes a weapon the carrying or possession of which is unlawful by such person under Part 2 or 3 of Article 4 of Chapter 11 of this title.

This law states that a person does not have to worry about being prosecuted for using force if it falls within the guidelines of the stated laws, unless, in a deadly force case, that person uses a weapon he or she is not authorized to carry or be in possession of one.

All of the laws stated on Use of Force pertain to every person in the State of Georgia except for OCGA 17-4-20.

POLICE USE OF FORCE

What I am going to expound on further is police Use of Force and how it is applied to this occupation according to my understanding and training. There are essentially six levels to police use of force and they are as follows:

1) **Officer Presence** – an officer in uniform and/or in a marked police unit, making his or her presence known in an area as a deterrent for crime

2) **Verbal Commands** – an officer telling someone to do something without making physical contact with the person

3) **Soft Hands** – this is when an officer makes physical contact, with a non-compliant person, in a way that is not overly invasive or forceful (escorting someone by the arm, holding someone back, etc.)

4) **Hard Hands** – this is when an officer makes contact with a non-compliant person in a forceful manner without using any tools (pushing, punching, kicking, slamming someone to the ground, etc.)

5) **Non-Lethal Force** – this is when an officer uses non-lethal tools on a non-compliant person, issued to the officer in order to gain compliance. Sometimes officers may have to use modified tools if the situation calls for that (issued tools – ASP

Baton, Taser, OC Spray; modified tools – broom stick, 2x4, brick)

6) **Deadly Force** – this is when an officer uses force, on a non-compliant person, knowing that it will cause serious bodily harm or death (firearm, shotgun, patrol rifle, patrol car, cutting tools)

Law Enforcement Officers find themselves in very dangerous and spontaneous situations that can occur at a moment's notice. In some instances, an officer only has seconds to assess and evaluate a situation then make a decision that could cause someone, or the officer, his or her life. In these types of situations, adrenaline is at its peak and the officer has to rely on his or her training and knowledge to make a decision.

With using force, there is no particular order in which an officer is required to use any of these levels and many of these levels can be combined. For example, if an officer observes an active fight at a mall, while approaching the altercation he or she can be yelling verbal commands like, "break it up", "police", or "stop fighting". As the officer gets closer, he or she can still give verbal commands while applying hard hands, grabbing someone and slamming him or her to the ground to break up the fight. The officer has the responsibility to control the scene and make an arrest with probable cause.

In other situations, the first five levels can be bypassed and an officer can go straight to deadly force. For example, a school police officer is walking the hallways in a school and sees a student pull a knife or gun out on another student. In that situation, the officer can use deadly force because deadly force has already been presented.

RESISTING

There are two types of resistance officers will encounter while employed. They are passive resistance and active resistance.

Passive Resistance – nonviolent opposition to authority, especially a refusal to cooperate with legal requirements.

Active Resistance – taking a physical action while refusing to accept or comply with something; the attempt to prevent something by action.

Passive resistance in policing is basically when a person is refusing to comply with lawful orders or commands but is not physically resisting the officer. For example, a suspect is told to leave an area after a verbal altercation. The suspect sits in a chair and tells the officers, "I'm not going any f*cking where!" The suspect is not resisting the officer physically but his or her non-compliance is viewed as passively resisting. Officers now have the option to exercise which type of force they will implement in order to gain compliance. In some situations, like this, a suspect can be taken into custody without incident. Sometimes, once physical contact is made with the suspect, the situation can go from passive to active resistance very quickly.

Passive resistance can be seen during unlawful protests when officers use OC Spray or gas in an attempt to disperse the crowd and regain order.

Active resistance in policing is basically when a person refuses to comply with the lawful orders or commands of officers and the officers now have to use physical force to gain compliance. For example, a suspect is told to leave an area after a verbal altercation and refuses. The officers approach the suspect and attempt to use soft hands to escort the suspect out of the location. The suspect snatches his arms away and pushes the escorting officer stating, "I ain't going no f*cking where!" This situation would more than likely lead to more officers arriving to back the initial officer. Their arrival can de-escalate the situation from active to passive resistance very quickly.

Using the same example of the protest, it can become active resistance when protestors start throwing items and charging the police to fight during the protest.

DE-ESCALATION

De-escalation – reduction of the intensity of a conflict or potentially violent situation.

De-escalation is a tool I use the most. Thankfully, I was blessed with the ability to get people to understand their current situation just by talking which leads to compliance in most of my cases. In a lot of situations, citizens are driven to take certain actions being led by their emotions. I have found that if I can get them to refocus on anything other than the source of their aggression, I can usually get people to calm down and regain their rationale when making decisions. This usually leads to voluntary compliance.

I have found that most people just want someone to vent to or talk to. There are others who don't really want to get into trouble but the heightened emotional state may cause them to think about doing something they know they will regret after they have calmed down.

Separation from the source of anger, relaxation breathing, walking, and other methods can be used to de-escalate a situation. The only groups that I have had problems with when de-escalating are people under the influence of alcohol or drugs, persons with severe mental illness, and juveniles. I have found that the rational part of their thought process does not always compute the seriousness of a given outcome when having to make good decisions.

I was trained that **<u>ONCE A SUSPECT IS IN HANDCUFFS, THE USE OF FORCE SITUATION IS OVER AND COMPLIANCE HAS BEEN GAINED!</u>**

DEADLY FORCE

Common questions I have heard many people ask when it comes to police using force are:

Why couldn't they shoot him in the arm?

Why did they have to shoot him? All he had was a knife!

Did it take that many officers to arrest him?

To address these and other questions like these, I will explain a few things based on how I was trained.

Additional officers show up to a scene to make sure the primary officer is ok and does not need help; for example, on a traffic stop. All communication is transmitted over the radios officers carry. When an officer goes out on a traffic stop, other officers are listening. They know the officer's location, what type of vehicle is pulled over, and sometimes how many people are in the car. Another officer or officers may go to the traffic stop just to make sure it is secure and check on the initiating officer. Most times it has nothing to do with the person or people in the vehicle.

There are situations where officers are alerted through the computer system of a possible high alert situation. The computer will alert other officers that the initiating officer may have stopped someone with a warrant (a wanted person), a stolen vehicle, known gang members with violent tendencies, and many other types of alerts. When this occurs, other officers will automatically converge on the initiating officer as back-up and for safety purposes.

Now the big issue… how and when an officer chooses to take physical action against a suspect, whether there are multiple officers retaining a subject or an officer using his or her firearm.

When it comes to using a firearm, I was trained to shoot to stop the threat, not shoot to kill. When a person looks at the human anatomy, the size of legs and arms are relatively small compared to the torso. To have the highest probability of stopping a threat, I was trained to aim at the largest part of the human body which is center mass of the human torso.

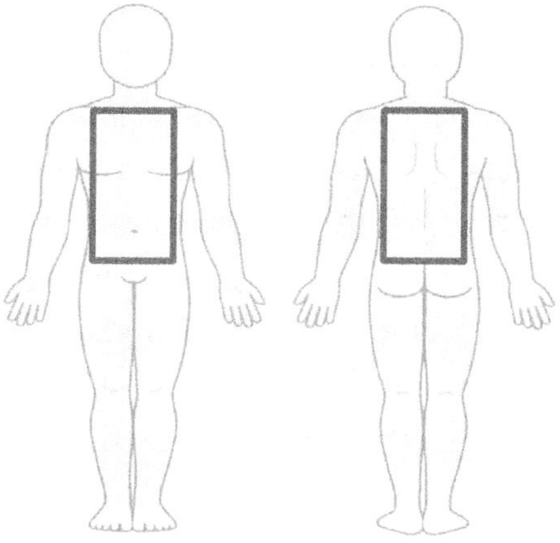

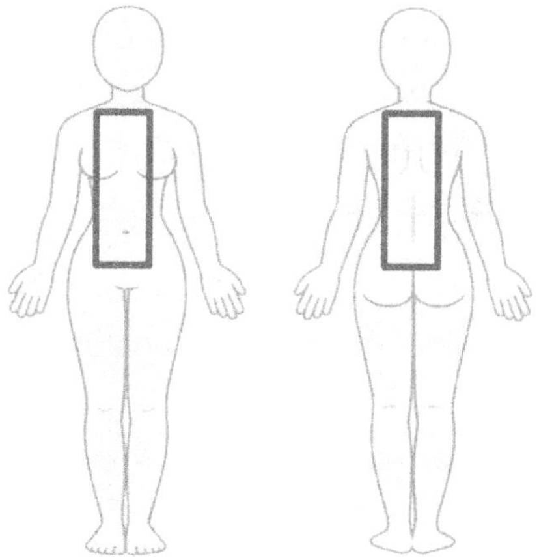

I was not trained to shoot suspects in the back. There are extreme situations where this may need to be done but it is highly irregular. Most people with their back turned to me do not pose a threat. An example of an extreme case could be, if a suspect refuses to comply with verbal commands from an officer. The suspect pulls a gun and turns away from the officers and starts running and firing at another person. I am not going to wait for the suspect to turn around to face me to stop him or her. I would use the same approach and fire center mass of the torso to stop the threat of the suspect trying to harm or kill someone else with the firearm. Another extreme case of shooting a suspect in the back would be if the suspect is running from an officer and while running, reaches back and starts firing at the pursuing officer.

As an officer, I was not trained to shoot at extremities like arms, hands, feet, and legs. ***I was told that there are two things a police officer never gets back: the words that come out of his or her mouth and the bullets that come out of his or her gun.***

Whenever an officer fires a weapon, he or she is responsible for where those bullets end up. If a suspect is in a heavily populated area and is holding a knife, threatening to assault someone, I am not going to aim for the arm, the hand, or the knife because the probability of hitting that small target and stopping the threat is very low. If I were to aim at the suspect's arm and miss, that bullet could end up striking and killing a bystander. I am now held accountable and responsible for that person's death. So, to increase my chances of stopping the threat of someone or myself receiving serious bodily harm or death from the suspect with the knife, I am going to aim at the largest part of the body which is center mass of the torso.

Secondly, I was taught that when a threat is presented I can either match the level of the threat or go a level above the presented threat. For example, if I am confident in my hand-to-hand fighting skills and someone is refusing to comply with a lawful order poses his or herself as a threat in a fighting stance, I can choose to fight that person hand-to-hand or go a level up using non-lethal tools issued to me (ASP Baton, OC Spray, or Taser). Another option in dealing with this threat is to call for more officers to back me up. My goal is to control the scene where I am and ultimately gain compliance from the suspect so I can stop the threat and affect an arrest when needed.

Finally, citizens have to understand that a gun is not the only tool in society that can be used to kill someone. Weapons like bats, hammers, 2x4's, pipes, poles, knives, cars, and chairs can all be used to inflict serious bodily injury and/or death to a person. Because these items and others can be used as deadly weapons, I am not going to allow a person to strike me or anyone else if I can prevent it. Pulling my department issued firearm out and using it in a situation where a serious threat with a weapon presents itself will be justified.

Now there are also situations where a person may not be armed but the use of a firearm can be justified in the defense of the officer. For example, an officer who is 5'4" and 135 pounds is in a situation where he or she has to defend his or herself against a suspect who is 6'4" and 225 pounds. With just his bare hands, that suspect could inflict serious bodily injury or death to the officer in a physical altercation. The officer could choose to use his or her firearm to stop the threat. In another situation, an officer is chasing a robbery suspect and during the chase the officer steps in a hole and breaks his or her leg. The suspect sees this and now doubles back to approach the downed officer in an aggressive manner; the officer could choose to use his or her firearm due to the disadvantaged position the officer is in.

What citizens need to understand is that in every police encounter, there is always going to be a gun present which is on the officer. Situations escalate and suspects can try to unarm an officer and use his or her firearm against the officer or other citizens. It is the officer's responsibility to make sure that does not happen at all costs. It is also the officer's responsibility to make sure the safety and security of life and property is protected. This includes the citizens and the officers alike.

This code section addresses defending a person's residence or dwelling.

<u>O.C.G.A. 16-3-23 Use of force in defense of habitation</u>: A person is justified in threatening or using force against another when and to the extent that he or she reasonably believes that such threat or force is necessary to prevent or

terminate such other's unlawful entry into or attack upon a habitation; however, such person is justified in the use of force which is intended or likely to cause death or great bodily harm only if:

(1) The entry is made or attempted in a violent and tumultuous manner and he or she reasonably believes that the entry is attempted or made for the purpose of assaulting or offering personal violence to any person dwelling or being therein and that such force is necessary to prevent the assault or offer of personal violence;

(2) That force is used against another person who is not a member of the family or household and who unlawfully and forcibly enters or has unlawfully and forcibly entered the residence and the person using such force knew or had reason to believe that an unlawful and forcible entry occurred; or

(3) The person using such force reasonably believes that the entry is made or attempted for the purpose of committing a felony therein and that such force is necessary to prevent the commission of the felony.

For contact, speaking opportunities, and book signings email me using djackenterprises@gmail.com!

@Redbird_Publications_LLC

@RedbirdPublicationsLLC

Keep up to date and stay in touch!

REFERENCES

Georgia Department of Community Affairs (2017). State of Georgia Tenant Landlord Handbook. https://www.dca.ga.gov/sites/default/files/georgia_landlord-tenant_handbook.pdf

Georgia Department of Education. (2004). Student Attendance Protocol. Polk School District Board of Education. https://www.gadoe.org/External-Affairs-and-Policy/Policy/Lists/Attendance/Attachments/107/715_StdAttnProt.pdf

Law Justia, https://law.justia.com/codes/georgia/2017/

Merriam-Webster Dictionary

Nelson, T. (2018). Minnesota Prosecutor Charges Sexting Teenage Girl With Child Pornography. ACLU of Minnesota

United States Department of Justice. (2017). Citizens Guide to U.S. Federal Law on Child Pornography. https://www.justice.gov/criminal-ceos/citizens-guide-us-federal-law-child-pornography

Made in the USA
Monee, IL
04 November 2026

67378979R00075